LUDWIG WITTGENSTEIN

MAKERS OF CONTEMPORARY THEOLOGY

EDITORS:

The Rev. Professor D. E. NINEHAM

The Rev. E. H. ROBERTSON

PAUL TILLICH, *by J. Heywood Thomas*

RUDOLF BULTMANN, *by Ian Henderson*

DIETRICH BONHOEFFER, *by E. H. Robertson*

TEILHARD DE CHARDIN, *by Bernard Towers*

MARTIN BUBER, *by Ronald Gregor Smith*

GABRIEL MARCEL, *by Sam Keen*

LUDWIG WITTGENSTEIN, *by W. D. Hudson*

MARTIN HEIDEGGER, *by John Macquarrie*

LUDWIG WITTGENSTEIN

The Bearing of his Philosophy upon Religious Belief

by

W. D. HUDSON

JOHN KNOX PRESS
RICHMOND, VIRGINIA

British edition published by the Lutterworth Press
4 Bouverie Street, London, England, 1968

American edition published by John Knox Press,
Richmond, Virginia, 1968

Library of Congress Catalog Card Number: 68-11971

First published 1968
Second printing 1968

Printed in the U.S.A.
24-0656

Contents

Foreword

I should like to express my thanks to two friends and colleagues, Professor D. J. O'Connor and Mr. S. G. Langford, with whom I have, from time to time, discussed some of the matters dealt with in the following pages. These discussions have helped me to formulate my own ideas more precisely. Professor O'Connor was also kind enough to read and comment on part of my script. I hardly need add that neither of those named should be assumed to share any opinion which I have expressed ; nor do they share the responsibility for any mistakes which I may have made.

W. D. H.

I

Introduction

WITTGENSTEIN would, I think, have been surprised, perhaps dismayed, to find himself included in a series entitled *Makers of Contemporary Theology*. He was not a theologian, but a philosopher. The passages in his published writings which refer explicitly to theology form a very small proportion of the whole. Nevertheless, anyone who wishes to acquire a contemporary understanding of theology ought to have some knowledge of his work.

He was preoccupied with the concept of *meaning*. Under what conditions is language meaningful, and under what, meaningless? His answers to this question were of the first importance and it is not too much to say that they have given its shape to philosophical thinking in this country for a generation.

Understanding Christian theology is, of course, largely a matter of finding out what theologians have said but it is also a matter of understanding what kind of talk their talk about God is. What is its logical structure? How is it related to other sorts of discourse, such as scientific theorizing or moral judgment? The most penetrating intellectual challenge which Christian believers have to meet in our day comes from those who call in question the meaningfulness of religious language. There is no point in discussing whether our beliefs are true or false, unless those beliefs make sense; and some modern philosophers have put up formidable arguments to the effect that they do not. In this brief, and of necessity all too sketchy study, we shall try to get clear some of the views which the most influential of modern philosophers expressed concerning meaning, and to give some indication of their bearing on theology and religious belief.

The reader must not expect to find here any new truths about God. Philosophers, or at any rate those of the contemporary analytical kind, are not concerned to bring new truths to light in the way that scientists, historians, or theologians are. In philosophy, as Wittgenstein put it, 'the problems are solved, not by giving new information, but by arranging what we have always known'.[1] What the philosopher tries to do is to show how the things we know are like, and how unlike, one another; and what it is to know what we know, or mean what we mean, or believe what we believe.

Neither must the reader, I am afraid, expect to find here light which will banish once for all his puzzlement about theology or religion. In philosophy, it always happens that, just when everything seems to have been tidily arranged, we begin to see that some things do not quite fit the places given to them. A capacity to be perplexed by, rather than rest content with, what is said is the measure of a capacity for philosophy. Lord Russell tells us that, soon after Wittgenstein came to Cambridge, he asked G. E. Moore whether the latter thought their new pupil a genius or a crank. Moore said that he thought Wittgenstein a genius. Russell asked why. (To appreciate the story, you need to know that Moore probably strove more assiduously than any other modern philosopher for simplicity of expression.) Moore replied: 'Because he's the only man who looks puzzled at my lectures !'[2]

Puzzlement persists, but from time to time the fog clears over particular perplexities. It is perhaps not too much to hope that this short study will enable the reader to get some issues concerning the meaning of theological or religious language into clearer focus and to understand a little better the nature of Christian belief.

2

Life [3]

LUDWIG JOSEF JOHANN WITTGENSTEIN was born in Vienna on 26th April, 1889, and, one of a large family, spent his childhood in his parents' palatial Viennese home and on their country estates. His father, a wealthy and cultured industrialist, was of Jewish descent but had embraced Protestant Christianity; his mother was a Roman Catholic and Wittgenstein himself was baptized in that Church. He was educated at home until he was fourteen, then went to school in Linz and subsequently to the Technische Hochschule in Berlin-Charlottenburg to study engineering. In 1908 he came to England to do research in aeronautics, but eventually his interest turned to logic and the philosophy of mathematics and he went to study these subjects in Cambridge with Bertrand Russell and G. E. Moore. His progress was spectacular and his teachers soon recognized his philosophical genius. Russell says that towards the end of Wittgenstein's first term in 1912, the latter asked, 'Am I a complete idiot or not? If I am, I shall be an aeronaut; if not, a philosopher'. In reply, Russell suggested that he should write a paper on some philosophical subject during the vacation. When he showed it to him, at the beginning of the new term, Russell read one sentence and then said, 'No. You must not be an aeronaut!' Both Russell and Moore have said that getting to know Wittgenstein was one of the most exciting intellectual adventures of their lives; and he was soon discussing philosophy with them on equal terms.

Having enlisted in the Austrian army in 1914, Wittgenstein continued to think about philosophical problems, recording his conclusions in notebooks which he carried in his knapsack. In 1918 he completed his first book, *Logisch-Philosophische*

Abhandlung published in a German-English parallel text as *Tractatus Logico-philosphicus* in 1922. We shall give some account of its main ideas below. Believing that he had solved all important philosophical problems in this work, Wittgenstein gave up philosophy and took a one year course at a teachers' training college before becoming a village schoolmaster in Trattenbach and other places from 1920-26. But he was temperamentally unsuited to the job and eventually had to give it up. He became a gardener at a monastery for a few months. This frugal, disciplined life appealed to him and he even contemplated taking up the monastic life permanently; but he could not share the beliefs on which it was based. Next, he spent two years designing a house for one of his relatives in Vienna.

Through the twenties, he kept in touch with some old Cambridge friends and with Moritz Schlick, professor of philosophy at Vienna and founder of the Vienna Circle, the group of philosophers, scientists and mathematicians who worked out what is known as Logical Positivism. Wittgenstein never joined the Circle but its members were greatly influenced by his *Tractatus*. In 1930 Wittgenstein was elected to a fellowship at Trinity College, Cambridge. He had grown dissatisfied wtih the *Tractatus*, believing it to be in fundamental respects mistaken, and during the next twenty years worked out his later philosophy. His interim ideas are to be found in the *Blue* and *Brown Books*, dictated to pupils in 1933-34 and 1934-35. His mature thoughts are found in *Philosophical Investigations*, completed in 1949 and published posthumously. Wittgenstein was elected to Moore's chair in 1939, but during the war he worked as a porter at Guy's Hospital, and then got a job in Newcastle making ointments. He resigned his chair in 1947 and died in 1951.

His personality was fascinatingly complex. He was solitary yet affectionate; absurdly offended if his views were misrepresented yet indifferent to all public honours; capable of giving away a fortune inherited from his father lest it interfere with his philosophy yet at times pettily quarrelsome; a man who devoted most of his days to academic study yet was so contemptuous of the academic life that he urged his pupils to avoid it at all costs. As a philosopher, he stands in the front rank beyond all question. Though some, like Russell, who admire his early work, think rather poorly of his later method of analysis, it would be hard to deny him the title which Mr. P. F. Strawson used in reviewing *Philosophical Investigations* – 'the first philosopher of the age'.[4]

3

Attitude to Religion

WITTGENSTEIN'S personal attitude to religion is difficult to define. We can only go by what his friends have said.[5] He certainly did not profess any specific creed or ally himself with any church. Referring to two of his pupils who had become Roman Catholics he said: 'I could not possibly bring myself to believe all the things that they believe'. But was this intended as a criticism of their beliefs or an acknowledgement of some defect within himself? Professor Malcolm, who records this remark, thinks that it was the latter.

Whilst visiting Swansea, Wittgenstein lodged with a Non-conformist minister (whom he chided for having so many unread books on his shelves, presumably put there only to impress his flock!). An old man, who called one day, said to Wittgenstein that Jesus Christ was the world's greatest philosopher. Wittgenstein tried to explain to him that Jesus Christ was not a philosopher at all; but he said afterwards that he understood why the old man wanted Christ to be the greatest of everything.

However hard it may be to say precisely what Wittgenstein's personal attitude to Christianity was, it seems certain that it changed from one of open hostility to something far removed from this. In his obituary notice on Wittgenstein for *Mind*, in 1951, Russell said 'He had been dogmatically anti-Christian, but in this respect he changed completely. The only thing he ever told me about this was that once in a village in Galicia during the war (1914-18) he found a bookshop containing only one book, which was Tolstoy, on the Gospels. He bought the book, and, according to him, it influenced him profoundly'. The book is generally believed to have been that translated into English under the title *What I Believe*.

Did Wittgenstein know anything at first hand of religious experience ? In a paper which he read at Cambridge in 1929 he claimed that he himself sometimes had 'the experience of feeling absolutely *safe*', continuing : 'I mean the state of mind in which one is inclined to say "I am safe, nothing can injure me *whatever* happens".' The ideas of Divine judgment, forgiveness and redemption also seem to have had some meaning for him. Malcolm says that he related them to feelings of disgust with himself, an intense desire for purity, and a sense of the helplessness of human beings to make themselves better. Wittgenstein also said that he thought the notion of immortality could acquire meaning through the feeling that one had duties from which not even death could release one.[6] So, if the elements of 'ultimate demand' and 'final succour' constitute, as H. H. Farmer has maintained,[7] the essence of religious experience, then Wittgenstein certainly appears to have had it to some degree. The author of a recent student of Wittgenstein, Dr. G. Pitcher, thinks it must have distressed him to find that, although he wanted and needed to believe in God, he could not do so.[8] But we do not know that Wittgenstein ever represented the situation to himself in these terms.

Did he believe that there is any point in trying to make out a rational case for religion ? According to Malcolm, he was impatient with all so-called proofs of the existence of God : 'When once I quoted to him a remark of Kierkegaard's to this effect : "How can it be that Christ does not exist, since I know that He has saved me?", Wittgenstein exclaimed: "You see! it isn't a question of *proving* anything!"'

Philosophical attempts to prove the existence of God take us into the realm of metaphysics and it is well-known that the type of philosophy with which Wittgenstein's name is commonly associated has, on the whole, not looked favourably on metaphysics. But what was his own attitude to metaphysics ? He once said : 'Don't think that I despise metaphysics or ridicule it. On the contrary, I regard the great metaphysical writings of the past as amongst the noblest productions of the human mind.'

Miss G. E. M. Anscombe, who knew him well, has said emphatically that, in interpreting Wittgenstein, we must not suppose that he worked from some initial doctrine about the impossibility of metaphysics; he had no such doctrine. Nevertheless, as we shall see, in his earlier work, at any rate, Wittgenstein put up what certainly appears to be an impressive argument against the possibility of metaphysics.

On his attitude to religion, Malcolm's conclusion seems to be near the mark: 'I do not wish to give the impression that Wittgenstein accepted any religious faith – he certainly did not – or that he was a religious person. But I think that there was in him, in some sense, the *possibility* of religion. I believe that he looked on religion as a 'form of life' (to use an expression from the *Investigations*) in which he did not participate, but with which he was sympathetic and which greatly interested him'. We shall be concerned with this concept of religion as a 'form of life' when we come to his later philosophy.

4

Earlier Thought

IN the *Tractatus*, Wittgenstein developed what is called his 'picture theory' of meaning. His basic idea was that the meaning of language is that to which it refers or, in a word, its referent: 'A name means an object. The object is its meaning'. (3.203).[9] We can indicate the latter either verbally or ostensively. If, for instance, anyone asks, 'What does "typewriter" mean?', we can reply with the definition: a machine for producing printed characters on paper as a substitute for handwriting; or we can take him and point a typewriter out to him. Whether verbally or ostensively, we are indicating the thing to which the word refers. There is much to be said for this view that the meaning of language is its referent, or, to put it in another way, that language is truth-functional.

It is important to be clear just what Wittgenstein was doing in the *Tractatus*. He was working out the *logic* of this view of meaning. What necessarily follows from it concerning language, and the world (or reality – for him the expressions were virtually interchangeable) to which language refers? Wittgenstein was not concerned, as a philologist or a physicist might have been, to show how, in fact, words are used or the world is made. His investigation was not empirical, but entirely logical. What, given that meaning is referent, *must* be the case in order for there to be meaning at all? That was what interested him; and so we find him speaking of the logical 'simples', i.e. 'names' and 'objects', of language and reality respectively, and shrugging off the request for examples of an actual name or object, with the rejoinder that it is not his business, as a logician, to supply them.[10]

Meaning as Determinate Referent

He made the point that meaning, to be meaning, must not only consist of a referent, or referents, but must be *determinate*. True, we may often not be able to determine the meaning of language, either because the words or signs which the speaker uses are unfamiliar to us, or because he is using familiar ones in vague or ambiguous ways. But the empirical possibility, that men may be unable to determine meaning, does not alter the logical necessity that if anything being said is meaningful, then its meaning must be determinate. It must, that is, be what it *is*, and not anything else. Otherwise, it would not simply be the case that we might sometimes not know what is meant; we *could not* know. I think this was the point which Wittgenstein was making when he wrote: 'A proposition has one and only one complete analysis' (3.25). There is, that is to say, something specific and determinate which is what any piece of *significant* discourse means. We may or may not be able, in fact, to get down to it; but it is nevertheless, so to say, there to be got down to. If it were not, it would be logically impossible to differentiate between meaningful and meaningless discourse.

Now, if meaning is referent and must be determinate, certain inferences can be drawn concerning (i) language and (ii) the world.

Wittgenstein's first inference is this: that all meaningful language must in the last analysis be reducible to what he called 'elementary propositions' (4.221). To see what he meant by 'elementary propositions', let us take a statement: 'The motor car is in the garage'. If the speaker's meaning is determinate, then he must be referring to one specific motor-car. But the expression, 'The motor-car', is a description and descriptions are general in the sense that they could conceivably fit more than one referent. However, to know what the speaker means we must know which particular motor-car is in the garage. What kind of motor-car is he referring to and which particular one of that kind? These questions are not answered by the statement

'The motor-car is in the garage' and yet they must be answerable if the speaker's meaning is determinate. And so, in order to get down to what the speaker really means, it is necessary to analyse the 'complex' proposition that the motor-car is in the garage into 'simpler' propositions which eliminate its indeterminateness. If, for instance, the motor-car intended is a Ford Zephyr, then a proposition, or propositions, will be needed which refer to that kind of automobile. But there are many Ford Zephyrs, so further analysis will be required to provide a proposition, or propositions, which make the reference to one Ford Zephyr quite determinate. The last constituent or constituents of such analysis, Wittgenstein maintained, must be one or more such elementary propositions.

He said that an elementary proposition is a 'concatenation of names' (4.22). It is important to notice that 'name' is a technical expression in the *Tractatus*. It was not proper names, as we commonly think of them (e.g. Smith), which he had in mind, but the 'logically proper names' of simple objects. A 'name', or 'simple sign', is a term which does not describe but designates, or denotes, that of which it is the name: and so it can refer to that and that alone. Propositions whose terms are verbally definable refer indirectly, i.e. *via* the propositions into which they can be analysed. But if propositions are meaningful, i.e. if they have determinate reference, then such verbal analysis must be terminable. It must *not* be logically possible to go on *ad infinitum* replacing propositions by propositions, words by other words. There must come a point where words refer directly to things, otherwise analysis can never bring us to the referents of the language we use and so never to what we *mean*. As Wittgenstein has it: 'The requirement that simple signs be possible is the requirement that sense be determinate' (3.23). So, it follows logically from his view of meaning that the ultimate constituents of language *must* be 'elementary propositions' and 'names'.

Wittgenstein's second inference concerned the world, or reality. It must consist, in the last analysis, of 'simple objects'.

These objects are 'simple' in the sense that the only way in which we can use language to refer to them is by naming them. We cannot, that is to say, describe them because that would only be possible if they were analysable in terms of constituents or properties – as, for instance, molecules are analysable in terms of atoms or things like tables in terms of their defining characteristics. Wittgenstein's point may be put like this : if meaning is referent and if it is determinate, then for there to be meaning at all there must necessarily be such simple objects to which language can refer. Just as it is necessary for language itself to be ultimately analysable into propositions which do not describe but name, because descriptions are always to some degree indeterminate, so it is logically necessary for the world, to which language refers, to consist, in the last analysis, of that which can only be named, not described, i.e. of simple objects.

Objects constitute 'the substance of the world' (2.021) said Wittgenstein, and he seems to have meant by 'object' much the same as Aristotle meant by 'first substance'. Substance on this view of the matter is a logical necessity. The substance of a thing is that in which all its attributes inhere. Everything which you can say about X (where X is anything about which statements can be made) is logically distinct from X-in-itself, the unknown substratum, the substance in reality, which corresponds to the substantive, 'X' in language. This is a classic example, of course, of drawing metaphysical conclusions from purely linguistic premises. The grammatical rule, in our syntax, that every sentence expressing a proposition must have a subject, is taken for a fact about reality itself – that every statement must in the last analysis, be about some substance. Wittgenstein is as guilty of this move from language to metaphysics as Aristotle was (which is, no doubt, one reason why, as we shall see, he called his own philosophy nonsense).

The point, at the moment, however, is that, because, in order to have a proposition, you must have a subject (which refers to a substance) *and* something more, namely a predicate, it is not surprising to find Wittgenstein saying that objects do not exist in isolation. He said: 'The world divides into facts' (1.2). He spoke of *Sachlagen* (situations), i.e. molecular facts; and of *Sachverhalten* (states of affairs), i.e. atomic facts into which the former can be analysed. An atomic fact is 'a combination of objects' (2.01). We see then that what he infers from his view of meaning concerning the world, parallels what he infers from it concerning language. Language reduces to 'elementary propositions' which consist of 'names': the world to 'states of affairs' which consist of 'objects'. The former pictures, models or represents, the latter.

The Picture Theory

Perhaps the best way of clarifying this 'picture theory' is to ask: what conditions must be fulfilled, according to Wittgenstein, if a proposition is to be, as he said it was, a logical picture of a situation? We find that there are three such conditions.[11]

First, the elements of the proposition must correspond one for one with the elements of the state of affairs, or atomic fact, represented. 'In a proposition there must be exactly as many distinguishable parts as in the situation that it represents' (4.04). Secondly, the features of the 'structure', or 'form', of the proposition must be paralleled one for one by those of the structure, or form, of the state of affairs. 'The configuration of objects in a situation corresponds to the configuration of simple signs in the propositional sign' (3.21). Thirdly, the proposition must be correlated by a 'law of projection' (4.0141) with the state of affairs which it represents: '...a proposition is a propositional sign in its projective relation to the world' (3.12).

Why are these conditions necessary? So far as the first is concerned, we saw that, for meaning to be determinate, meaningful propositions must consist, in the last analysis of simples which refer to simples, i.e. of names which refer to objects. An elementary proposition consists of names only and it can therefore only picture an atomic fact, which consists of objects, if, for every object, there is a name and *vice versa*. If we draw a picture which purports to be a picture of a glass and a jug on a tray, then, *pace* some modern artists, there must be in the picture representations of a glass, a jug and a tray.

Regarding the second condition, we need to recognise that a mere list of names cannot represent a state of affairs. Said Wittgenstein: 'Only facts express a sense, a set of names cannot' (3.142). It is the *fact* of the proposition, i.e. the fact of its elements having the configuration, the structure, the form, which they do have, corresponding to the fact that the elements of the state of affairs have an identical configuration, structure or form, which constitutes the picture (see 3.1432)[12]. The importance which Wittgenstein attached to the *fact* of the proposition, as a configuration, is seen to be justified if, to turn again to the illustration of a moment ago, we note that it is not merely the drawings of a glass, and a jug, and a tray respectively which picture a glass and jug on a tray, because if we put these three drawings one after another along a line they would not picture that. They must be *arranged* in the picture as what they represent is arranged in reality.

To appreciate the third condition of the picture theory – that the proposition must be correlated by a 'law of projection' with the state of affairs which it pictures – we must be clear, first, about the difference between a proposition and a propositional sign. The latter is the sentence, spoken or written, which expresses the proposition. 'The cat is on the mat' is a propositional sign. We could say that it consists of six words. But we could not say that the proposition that the cat is on the mat, does so. The proposition does not consist of words at all: they merely express it. However, Wittgenstein did not wish to postulate mysterious metaphysical entities, i.e. propositions, distinct from their signs; he thought it would be enough to say that 'a proposition is a propositional sign in its projective relation to the world' (3.12). It is, that is to say, a sentence intended or understood as referring to reality. It is so intended or understood when the elements of the propositional sign (in the last analysis, the words of the elementary propositional signs, into which the complex propositional sign may be broken down) are related by laws, or rules, of projection with the elements in reality (in the last analysis, objects) to which they refer. When so related these words (or signs) become the names (or symbols) of the proposition. Wittgenstein had a rather complicated illustration of what he meant by 'a law of projection' (see 4.014 and 4.0141), but I think that the idea is really quite simple. To take his example, or part of it, there are rules for projecting musical sounds from a musical score, and, if you know what these are, then you know, from looking at the score, what the piece of music is which it represents. So in a propositional sign, such as 'The cat is on the mat' (to take 'cat' and 'mat', as though they were names of Wittgensteinian 'objects' which they are not) there are rules correlating the signs 'cat' and 'mat' with the objects, cat and mat, respectively, and by intending the signs to have that reference, in the particular configuration which they have in this propositional sign, you 'think the sense of the proposition (3.11) i.e. you think the state of affairs which it pictures.

Reference and Sense

We must now notice differences in the way that names and propositions respectively refer. For one thing, a proposition is not meaningless if it is false. 'Edinburgh is the capital of England' is not nonsense in the way that 'Hgrubnide si eht latipac fo dnalgne' is. The former is meaningful but untrue : it is a possible picture of a situation, but there is, in fact no such situation. But, unlike propositions, names which have no referents are meaningless. For instance, 'Ipe' is meaningless, understood as a name, if there is no such person or thing as Ipe in fact or fiction.

If I utter a name which you have never previously encountered, such as 'Ipe', then, before you can know what I mean (i.e. to what I am referring) you must ask 'Who or what is Ipe ?' and I must tell you. But suppose I utter a proposition which you have never heard before, e.g. 'Wittgenstein once thought of becoming a professional musician', then, provided you know to whom or what the names in the last analysis of the proposition refer, I do not have to tell you to what fact, or putative fact, the proposition refers before you can understand it. In uttering the proposition, I have already done so.

To mark this difference between names and propositions, Wittgenstein said that names have *Bedeutung* (which may be translated 'reference') and elementary propositions *Sinn* (which may be translated 'sense'). The underlying notion of meaning as referent is common to both, but the difference is brought out by these different terms. As Wittgenstein put it: 'The meanings (*Bedeutungen*) of simple signs (words) must be explained to us, if we are to understand them. With propositions, however, we make ourselves understood. It belongs to the essence of a proposition that it should be able to communicate a *new* sense (*Sinn*) to us' (4.026, 4.027).

In his earliest recorded remark about what has become known as his picture theory, Wittgenstein said: 'In the proposition a world is, as it were, constructed experimentally. (As when in the law-court in Paris a motor-car accident is represented by means of dolls, etc.)'[13] This explains how a proposition could be meaningful though false. The proposition is an 'experiment'. The 'picture' is presented and has meaning. Whether it is true or false – whether the experiment is successful or unsuccessful – is seen only by comparing it with reality. For it to be meaningful, you must know what it would be like for a proposition to be true or false,[14] but *not* necessarily which it is.

A proposition can convey a new sense to us, according to Wittgenstein, because the *sense* of the proposition lies in the fact that its elements (names) have a certain structure corresponding to the structure of the elements (objects) of the possible state of affairs, or situation, which it pictures (cf. 3.143-3.1432). In the proposition we can take what he calls here 'old expressions', (i.e. names of which the referents are known to us) and put them together in a new structure to form a 'new sense' (cf. 4.03). Though he thought that 'the world divides into facts' (1.2) he recognized that the facts may change, even though some more fundamental constituents of reality (objects) do not: 'Objects are what is unalterable and subsistent; their configuration is what is changing and unstable' (2.0271).

Logical Constants

There is one further point about the picture theory which we must note. Wittgenstein, in one place, said that it was his 'fundamental' idea that 'logical constants' are 'not representatives' (4.0312). By 'logical constants' he meant connective words such as 'not', 'and', 'or', 'if-then'. His point was that these words do not name objects as other 'non-logical' words do. Why did he think that? To take 'not' as our example, if 'not' named an object, then to say 'not not p' would be to say something different from 'p'; it would picture a situation which had two more objects (not, not) in it than the situation which 'p' pictured. But, taking it for granted that 'not not p' is materially equivalent to (i.e. has the same truth value as, or pictures the same situation as) 'p', Wittgenstein concluded that 'not' cannot logically refer to an object.

Why was this 'fundamental'? We saw at the beginning of this section that his basic idea was that all propositions are truth-functions of elementary propositions; that is to say, that any complex proposition can be broken down, in the last analysis, into propositions consisting only of names of objects, and the truth or falsity of the complex proposition depends upon whether the atomic facts, or states of affairs, to which these refer do, or do not, exist. Now, take a proposition such as (A) 'Tom is in the house and Mary is in the garden'. There is a logical constant here, namely 'and'. The proposition can be broken down into two simpler propositions: (A1) 'Tom is in the house', and (A2) 'Mary is in the garden'. If A1 is true and A2 is true, then A is true. If either A1 or A2 is false, or both are, then A is false. So the truth-value of A depends *only* on the truth-values of A1 and A2. The two propositions are connected by 'and', but *because* 'and' is not 'representative', we do not need to know the truth-value of 'and', as distinct from that of A1 or A2, in order to know whether 'A1 and A2' is true or false.

The theory of meaning which Wittgenstein worked out in the *Tractatus* was a remarkable logical achievement. We have been able to give only the most summary account of it and with its detailed philosophical examination we cannot concern ourselves here.[15] Our interest in it lies mainly in what follows from it concerning metaphysics, theology or religious belief and ethics. The logical positivists were the first who attempted to work this out. We must therefore now consider their views, and ask how far, if at all, they differed from Wittgenstein. We must then judge for ourselves the view, which is common to both them and him, that metaphysics, religious belief, theology and ethics belong to the realm of 'what cannot be said!'

5

'What Cannot be Said'

Logical Positivism

THE principal tenet of the logical positivists was that known as the verification principle. According to the earliest formulations of it, the meaning of a statement is the method of its verification. But what the principle amounts to can perhaps be better seen from the formulation given to it by Professor A. J. Ayer, the leading British exponent of logical positivism. 'A statement is held to be literally meaningful if, and only if, it is either analytic or empirically verifiable'.[16] By 'literally meaningful' he meant capable of being shown to be true or false.

An analytic statement is one which can be shown to be true or false merely by appeal to the definitions of the signs or terms used in it, e.g. 'A brother is a male sibling'. If true, analytic statements are tautologies; if false, contradictions. The logical positivists held that all mathematical and logical statements are analytic. As such they are not factually informative. If true and tautologous, they are compatible with *any* state of affairs whatever; if false and contradictory, with *none* whatever.

The main import of the verification principle was that testability by empirical observation is the necessary and sufficient condition of meaningfulness in all but analytic statements. The logical positivists contended that all significant factual propositions can, in principle if not always in practice, be tested for truth or falsity empirically, i.e. by the evidence of our physical senses. They are all really hypotheses concerning future experience. If I say, 'There is a table in that room', I am predicting that any normal person will, under certain conditions, have certain experiences : he will, if he goes into the room, see or feel what is called a table. Even if my statement were about the past, e.g. 'There used to be a table in that room' it would be, nonetheless, a hypothesis concerning future experience : it would, in effect, predict what anyone would experience who set out to test it by, for instance, looking up old inventories of the furniture or consulting people who used to live in the room.

Two important questions arise concerning the verification principle. First : what is its correct formulation ? The problem has been to find a formulation which is neither too exclusive nor too inclusive. A scientific law of nature is a universal proposition, of the form 'All A's are B', and such a proposition cannot be verified by any finite number of empirical observations because it is always conceivable that there are A's, not hitherto observed, which are not B. It would seem to follow, on the verification principle, that scientific laws are therefore meaningless since they cannot be empirically verified. But the last thing the logical positivists wanted to do was to *exclude* the general laws of science as meaningless. To meet this difficulty about scientific laws, Ayer gave it as the mark of a genuine factual proposition, not that it should be equivalent to a finite number of observation statements, but simply that some observation statement could be deduced from it in conjunction with certain other premises without being deducible from these other premises alone. But it has been pointed out that this formulation would be met in such an example as the following. Let 'God created the world' be a putatively factual proposition and use the observation statement 'This is black'. Then, 'This is black' (observation statement) can be deduced from 'God created the world' (putatively factual proposition) together with 'If God created the world, then this is black' (another premise) without being deducible from this latter premise alone. Therefore, according to this rendering of the verification principle, 'God created the world' would be a significant factual proposition.[17] But no logical positivist wanted a criterion which would *include* statements about God as meaningful. I do not think that, in fact, a formulation of their verification principle, entirely satisfactory to logical positivists, has ever been found.

The second important question concerning the verification principle is : what is its precise status ? It is a definition of meaning, obviously, but what kind of definition ? Clearly, it is not a *lexical* or *reportive* definition. As 'meaning' is normally used, it would be absurd to say that statements about God, for instance, are meaningless. The logical positivists, or some of them, recognized this; and they had certainly not arrived at their definition simply by listening to the way in which people actually used the word 'meaning'. Their definition must, then, be *stipulative* : that is, it must represent a convention which they adopted and wished others to adopt. The convention was not, however, entirely arbitrary. As Ayer claimed, what the positivists took meaning to be, on the one hand, accurately described the criterion by which the truth or falsity of statements in common sense, natural science and history, is established; and on the other, provided a convincing account of the way in which logical or mathematical statements actually function.[18]

Turning to Wittgenstein, we find, in the *Tractatus*, something very similar to the logical positivists' verification principle. His basic position, it will be remembered, was that the meaning, or sense, of a proposition is the atomic fact, or facts, which it pictures. It follows, as he put it, that 'to understand a proposition is to know what is the case, if it is true' (4.024): in other words, what it pictures. So a proposition is understandable, i.e. has meaning, if, and only if, we know what would verify it : " . . . in order to be able to say ' "p" is true (or false)', I must have determined in what circumstances I call 'p' true, and in so doing I determine the sense (*Sinn*) of the proposition" (4.063). In order to verify it, 'we must compare it with reality' (2.223).

There is, however, room for doubt as to whether the parallel between Wittgenstein and the logical positivists is really as close as may appear. Did Wittgenstein imply, in speaking of comparison with reality, that the elements of reality must be

empirically observable? Some have argued that he did;[19] others
that he did not.[20] It is certainly possible that he intended his
criterion of meaning to be entirely formal, and tenable whether
one held the reality pictured in language to be empirically
observable or not. The logical positivists added to Wittgenstein's
logical analysis of meaning an empiricist theory of knowledge,
but the empiricism is not necessarily implied by his analysis.

The Rejection of Metaphysics

The logical positivists claimed that metaphysical statements –
with which they included theology and ethics – are meaningless
because (i) they do not purport to be analytic, and (ii) they
cannot be verified, or falsified, by sensory experience. Take, as an
example, 'God exists'. Most theists would not wish to take this
as analytic and true simply by definition of 'God' as 'one who
exists'. Even if we make it true by so defining 'God', the
question remains as to whether there is, in reality, any application for this word 'God'. But, taking 'God exists' as more than
analytic, is it empirically testable? If theists define God as one
who transcends the world of our experience, then in so far as it is
this God whom they have in mind, it would seem that 'God
exists' could not (logically) be verified or falsified by our
experience. By the verification principle, then, 'God exists'
seems to be literally meaningless.

As for ethical judgments such as 'Lying is wrong' or 'You
ought not to lie', though these have the syntactical appearance
of significant factual statements, the logical positivists held
that they are not what they appear to be. Wrongness is not a
property which can be observed by any physical sense; and we
cannot see that someone is under an obligation as we can that
he is under a tree. Therefore, they contended that a statement
such as 'Lying is wrong' is really an emotive ejaculation of
disgust with lying, equivalent to 'Lying-ugh!'; and 'You
ought not to lie' is really an imperative, equivalent to 'Don't
lie!'

Ayer did, indeed, concede that all which strictly follows from the verification principle is that metaphysical, theological or ethical propositions are *different* in meaning from empirical or analytic ones, not that they are necessarily meaningless. It may make some kind of sense to speak here of poetic or emotive meaning, as distinct from literal. But, he added, as he was perfectly entitled to do, that metaphysicians, theologians and moralists are deceived, if they suppose that they are doing the same work as scientists, only doing it more profoundly; and insisted, as he was also entitled to do, that, if this is *not* what they are doing, then it is up to them to give some plausible account of what they *are* doing.[21] In particular, they must explain what they mean by calling their statements 'factual', or saying that they contribute to knowledge, since the conditions for the significant use of either 'fact' or 'knowledge' in metaphysics, theology or ethics must be different from those in natural science.

Given the validity of their verification principle, the logical positivists' rejection of metaphysics is clear and self-consistent. Wittgenstein's treatment of the subject in the *Tractatus* is by no means so straightforward. He certainly consigns metaphysics, theology and ethics to the realm of 'what cannot be said'; but exactly what this implies is not so plain to see. We must try to analyse his argument stage by stage.

First, what are his grounds for designating metaphysical propositions non-significant? I think that he had two such grounds at least. (i) One was a principle that, in order to conceive of a proposition as true, we must be able to conceive of it also as false – or, to put the point another way, a proposition is meaningful, if and only if its negation, or denial, is meaningful. Whatever kind of proposition it is, and however simple or complex – whether it be 'Grass is green' or 'God is love' – we cannot understand what it means to say that such is the case, unless we can understand what it means to say that such is not the case. (ii) Wittgenstein's second ground for rejecting metaphysics was a principle that the limits of our language are the limits of our world and *vice versa*. A word or two, explaining how each of these principles applies to metaphysics will make the position clearer.

According to the former principle, if a proposition is significant, so is its negation. We saw that Wittgenstein held that 'to understand a proposition is to know what is the case if it is true' (4.024). To recognize the case if it is true, I must be able to differentiate this from the case if it is *not* true. I must therefore be able to conceive of its being false; its negation must be significant in that sense. This is what I take Wittgenstein to have meant when he wrote in his *Notebook*: 'In order for a proposition to be capable of being true, it must also be capable of being false';[22] and, in the *Tractatus*, 'The positive *proposition* necessarily presupposes the existence of the negative proposition and *vice versa*' (5.5151). Now, the trouble with metaphysical statements is that they are not significantly negatable in this way.

Suppose we make a metaphysical statement about ultimate reality – what Wittgenstein called 'objects' – such as 'Objects a, b, c, exist'. The negation of this will be 'It is not the case that objects a, b, c exist'. This negation, if significant, is capable of being true or false. But, if it is true, then its terms 'a', 'b', 'c', cannot refer to objects, because the truth of the proposition is that there are no such objects. So, on Wittgenstein's theory of meaning, these terms – 'a', 'b', 'c' – are meaningless and the proposition which contains them is meaningless also. Then by the first principle, on which Wittgenstein rejected metaphysics, that of significant negatability, the proposition ('Objects a, b, c, exist'), which this meaningless proposition ('Objects a, b, c, do not exist') negates, will be meaningless as well. If it cannot be meaningfully negated, it is not meaningful. The point is that metaphical propositions *all* purport to be about ultimate reality (they are about what Wittgenstein would have called 'objects') and so they fall foul of this objection (cf. 4.1272).

Now to the principle that the limits of language are the limits of the world and *vice versa* (cf. 5.6). Because language is significant only in so far as it pictures reality, it cannot, so to say, get beyond, or outside of, reality for then it would have nothing to picture. As Wittgenstein put it: 'So we cannot say in logic "The world has this in it, and this, but not that" '. Why? 'For that would appear to presuppose that we were excluding certain possibilities, and this cannot be the case, since it would require that logic should go beyond the limits of the world; for only in that way could it view those limits from the other side as well' (5.61). This seems to be perfectly valid, given Wittgenstein's theory of meaning. On that theory, we cannot talk about what we cannot picture; and we cannot picture what is beyond reality. So we cannot say that 'X is beyond (i.e. is not) reality'. But here the two principles come together, for, in that case, neither can we say 'X is reality', since, to be significant, this latter must be significantly negatable.

Having seen something of Wittgenstein's grounds for rejecting metaphysics, we must notice, secondly, that a great deal of the *Tractatus* itself is metaphysical in that it purports to be about ultimate reality, e.g. 'Objects make up the substance of the world' (2.021). But more, a great deal of the *Tractatus* is about the conditions which propositions must fulfil in order to be significant, e.g. we read: 'What any picture, of whatever form, must have in common with reality, in order to be able to depict it – correctly or incorrectly – in any way at all, is logical form, i.e. the form of reality' (2.18). This is a central thesis of the picture theory: the need for identity of structure between language and reality. But a statement of the conditions of significance in significant propositions cannot (logically) be itself a significant proposition in the same sense of 'significant' – just as a rule defining what counts as a goal or a move in such a game as football or chess is not itself a goal or move in that game. So it seems that, not only in occasional remarks about objects, but in its whole discussion of meaning – in everything which could be called its philosophy – the *Tractatus* goes beyond what can significantly be said! Wittgenstein did not shirk this conclusion. He wrote: 'My propositions serve as elucidations in the

following way : anyone who understands me eventually recog-
nizes them as nonsensical, when he has used them – as steps – to
climb up beyond them. (He must, so to speak, throw away the
ladder after he has climbed up it). He must transcend these
propositions, and then he will see the world aright !' (6.54).
The *Tractatus* is nonsense and its point is to reveal this fact !
A conclusion which, as Russell rightly remarked, leaves one
'with a certain sense of intellectual discomfort !'[23]

A third point which we must notice is that, though he held
that there are no significant philosophical propositions (in the
sense that 'philosophy is not a body of doctrine'), Wittgenstein
nevertheless thought that philosophy is an important and useful
'activity' (4.112). He said that it can, for instance, effect 'the
logical clarification of thoughts' (4.112), by which presumably
he meant the analysis of complex into elementary propositions.
Again, it can show that many of the problems which have
worried philosophers arise 'from our failure to understand the
logic of our language' (4.003: cf. 6.53). What he had in mind
here were clearly problems concerning metaphysics, theology
and ethics ; and he said that the way to solve such problems is to
see that they do not really arise. 'The solution of the problem . . .
is seen in the vanishing of the problem' (6.521).

The fourth point to get clear is just what view Wittgenstein
took of ethics and theology. On ethics he wrote : 'If there is any
value that does have value, it must lie outside the whole sphere
of what happens and is the case' (6.41). 'Ethics is transcendental'
(6.421) in that sense. If ethics is concerned with anything, it is
concerned with moral value, i.e. with what *ought* to be the case.
Now, on Wittgenstein's picture theory, meaningful language
mirrors what *is* the case. This is logically quite distinct from
what *ought* to be the case. So ethics lies beyond meaningful
language. Wittgenstein would have thought it a mistake to
argue, as intuitionists have done, that 'Lying is wrong', for
example, mirrors reality in much the same way as 'Poppies are
red', the only difference being that wrongness is not a natural
property like redness, but a 'non-natural' one. On theology, we

read in the *Tractatus* : '*How* things are in the world is a matter of complete indifference for what is higher. God does not reveal himself *in* the world' (6.432). This is not, of course, a declaration of belief in a God who does not care about the world or reveal himself in it.   The point is that God, *inasmuch as he is deemed to be transcendent*, cannot do so. 'The world is all that is the case'(1) ; so, propositions about a God who transcends the world cannot be pictures of what *is* the case. They must therefore be beyond what can meaningfully be said. Complicated as all this sounds, it is really quite simple and logical. Ethics is about what *ought* to be and what ought to be is *not* what is. God, as transcendent, is beyond the world, and what is beyond the world is *not* the world. Language is meaningful – on the picture theory – if, and only if, it mirrors the *world* which *is*. But this condition cannot (logically) be fulfilled by language concerning what is *not* the world (as a transcendent God is not the world) or concerning what is *not* that which is (as what ought to be is not that which is).

Finally, we find that Wittgenstein spoke of 'the mystical' – which was his expression for the realm of 'what cannot be said' – 'making itself manifest' (6.522). The problem is to know what he meant by this. The content of 'the mystical' appears to have been, in his view, twofold. First there are the rules of significance which constituted his own philosophy of meaning and which, for reasons noticed above, lie beyond what can significantly be said. By saying that 'the mystical' in this sense 'makes itself manifest', he may have meant that reflection on language brings us to see that these rules are the conditions of its being meaningful. Secondly, 'the mystical' is metaphysics, theology, ethics, etc. In what he says on these subjects, Wittgenstein was perhaps doing what is now called 'revisionary metaphysics'. Professor Max Black has argued : Wittgenstein is 'trying out a new way of looking at the world, which forces him to twist and bend language to the expression of his new thoughts (*sc.* thoughts about ethics, etc.). His own conclusion that the new vision is incoherent was a result that had to be won by severe mental labour, and could not have been achieved by any short-cut –

such as the automatic application of some principle of veri-
fiability. A negative metaphysics, such as that of the *Tractatus*,
has its own rules of procedure: the ladder must be *used* before
it can be thrown away'.[24] But if this is the only significance to be
found in his tantalizingly brief discussion of ethics, God, etc.,
why does he speak of 'the mystical' as 'making itself manifest'
and as 'existing'? (6.522). I suppose it may, in some sense,
'make itself manifest' as, in Black's words, a 'new vision', albeit
'incoherent'. But when Wittgenstein says: 'There are, indeed,
things which cannot be put into words. *They make themselves
manifest*. They are what is mystical' (6.522), this does seem to
imply something more. In some sense, Wittgenstein certainly
seems to have thought of 'the mystical' as existing. But in what
sense it is hard to say.

Wittgenstein said of metaphysical, theological and ethical
problems: 'it is not the solution of any problems of natural
science that is required' (6.4312). He also said that 'philosophy
sets limits to the much disputed sphere of natural science'
(4.113). It is tempting to jump to the conclusion, from remarks
such as these, that all he wished to do in the *Tractatus* was to
draw the logical 'map' of scientific discourse, differentiating it
from other kinds of discourse but not necessarily denying the
significance of the latter. But, however compatible such a view
may be with his later philosophy, we cannot, with any assurance,
so interpret the *Tractatus*. It seems that, in his early thought, he
took meaning *qua* meaning to be such that 'the mystical' cannot
meaningfully be discussed. His concluding remark on the
subject is: 'What we cannot speak about we must pass over in
silence' (7). But it is perhaps indicative of a difference between
him and them that the logical positivists felt it necessary to
criticize this remark on the ground that it implies that there is
something to be silent about.

Before turning to Wittgenstein's later thought, we will consider briefly two objections to religious belief and theology,
recently put up by modern philosophers, which are closely
related to his two grounds for rejecting metaphysics.

Theology and Falsification

One of Wittgenstein's grounds for rejecting metaphysics was the principle of significant negatability, and one objection brought against religious or theological propositions is that they are not falsifiable. There is a well-known essay of Professor A. Flew's entitled, 'Theology and Falsification', in which he uses a parable.[25] Two men argue about an overgrown garden. One says that a gardener comes and tends it; the other denies this. They never see or hear the gardener; they cannot pick up his scent with bloodhounds or trap him when they build an electric-wire fence round the garden. Nevertheless, the believer maintains that 'there is a gardener, invisible, intangible, insensible to electric shocks, a gardener who has no scent and makes no sound, a gardener who comes secretly to look after the garden he loves'. The unbeliever replies : but how does such a gardener differ from an imaginary gardener, or from no gardener at all ? The parallel with belief in a loving God, who rules this world, in which good and evil exist, is obvious.

Flew points out that 'to assert that such and such is the case is necessarily equivalent to denying that such and such is not the case'; (and in a footnote he says that what he means is that p is materially equivalent to – i.e. has the same truth values as – not-not-p). Next, he draws out the inference from this, that 'if there is nothing which a putative assertion denies then there is nothing which it asserts either ; and so it is not really an assertion'. The believer must therefore be prepared to answer the question : 'What would have to occur or to have occurred to constitute for you a disproof of the love of, or of the existence of, God ?' But it seems to be definitive of religious belief that believers should not give it up, whatever happens. So, either belief is unfalsifiable and therefore meaningless ; or it is falsifiable and therefore not religious.

Now I think four points can be educed from this argument. (i) p is materially equivalent to not-not-p. This is a purely formal point and follows from the rule for the use of 'not', consistently applied. In the case of religion, all it amounts to is, that such a statement as 'God loves us' has the same truth-value as 'It is not the case that God does not love us'. I cannot see any reason whatever why a believer should not agree. (ii) In order to understand the statement 'p is true', one must (logically) understand the statement 'p is not true'. We can (logically) only understand what it is for something to be true, if we also understand how its being true is different from its *not* being true. So : 'if there is nothing which a putative assertion denies then there is nothing which it asserts either'. Once more, I think the religious believer can readily agree ; for what this amounts to is simply that if a man understands 'God loves us' he must also be able to understand 'God does not love us'. These first two points are applications of Wittgenstein's principle of significant negatability. Flew seems, in effect, to be making a third point which is also in accordance with the *Tractatus*. (iii) It is possible to make 'God loves us' true by definition. If the word 'God' is defined as 'one who loves us', then 'God loves us' is tautologous and to deny that God loves us will be self-contradictory. But the point is that believers claim for their beliefs more-than-logical truth, and this being so, they must show them to be true by something more than appeal to a definition of the word 'God'. Here again, I can see no reason why believers should not agree.[26] (iv) But now to the rub ! Flew takes it for granted that all to which believers can appeal is events or circumstances, empirically observable in this present spatio-temporal world. In other words, a religious or theological proposition, if it is to have more-than-logical truth must, in his view, be empirically falsifiable in exactly the way that the hypotheses of natural science are.

On these four points the following comments seem relevant.

(i) The fourth point does not necessarily follow from the first three.

(ii) The first three are, as we have seen, in line with the thought of the *Tractatus*, but though the fourth is the corner-stone of logical positivism, it is by no means certain that it had any place in Wittgenstein's system.

(iii) The first three points follow from the definitions of the terms used in them. If anyone denied that: (a) p is materially equivalent to not-not-p, or (b) that to understand 'p is true', one must understand how its being true differs from its not being true, or (c) that to justify a claim to more-than-logical truth, one must appeal to more than definitions; then we should conclude that he did not know the meanings of some of the words here used, such as 'materially equivalent', 'not', 'understand', 'justify', 'logical', 'more-than-logical', etc. He could not use these expressions, in their normal senses, and utter his denial without self-contradiction. But when we come to the fourth point, it is by no means clear that anyone who denied that empirical falsifiability is the necessary and sufficient condition of literal or factual meaning could be said either not to know the normal senses of 'meaning', 'literal', 'factual', or to be contradicting himself.

(iv) However, in connexion with the second of the four points, it is relevant to ask: how can we know how a statement's being true differs from its not being true, if the statement is about what lies beyond our present experience? It has seemed to some religious thinkers that there is no answer to this question and therefore, if they wish to claim that their beliefs about God are true, they must show that these are not about what lies beyond our present experience. Mr. David Cox,[27] for instance, argued that every essential Christian belief can, and should, be restated in terms of human experience. The word 'God', he said, should be restricted by rule to contexts which describe the human experiences called 'meeting, encountering or knowing God'. Then such a statement as 'God exists' becomes the empirically testable hypothesis: 'some men and women have had, and all may have, experiences called "meeting God"'. God cannot, of course, be observed by physical sense, but Cox claimed that even Ayer had conceded that there are human experiences other than those of physical sense. He also maintained that Christian doctrines were originally framed to give expression to experience and, in the history of the Church, heretical doctrines have always been exposed as such by appeal to experience; so there is nothing new in his own attempt to put the 'religious hypothesis' on the same footing as any scientific hypothesis.

(v) But for a number of reasons Cox's attempt fails. To take only one here, scientists, as such, deduce from their hypotheses precise empirically observable predictions concerning the future course of events, and if these are falsified, surrender the hypothesis (or at least this is ideally what they do). If 'some men and women have had, and all may have, experiences called "meeting God"' is to be treated as though it were a scientific hypothesis then what is meant by 'meeting God' and the circumstances in which this experience will definitely occur must be stated *quite precisely* and if the prediction proves false, the hypothesis abandoned. Now, however firm their conviction, can Christian advocates in fact make such precise predictions? If the predictions which they do make about the experiences which their hearers will have, when they turn to Christ, are unfulfilled, do they abandon their beliefs? I am not saying that they should; what I am saying is that the believer cannot have it *both* ways – he cannot claim that his belief is, in effect, empirically testable like a scientific hypothesis, and then claim, if his predictions go unfulfilled, that he is nonetheless entitled to retain his belief.

(vi) If we can form no idea of how a religious belief's being true would differ from its not being true, then it would seem to be impossible to know what is meant by this belief. But its truth or falsity need not be capable of being established by our experience here and now. It is, true enough, the mark of a scientist, as such, that he does not save his hypothesis by claiming that, although it appears to be falsified now, it will be seen to be true hereafter. But it does not follow that, unless the religious believer, in this respect, treats his beliefs as the scientist treats his hypotheses, everything he says about these beliefs must be meaningless (unless, of course, we make it follow, as the logical positivists did, by a stipulative definition of 'meaning').

The Problem of Transcendence

We saw that Wittgenstein's second ground for rejecting metaphysics, theology and ethics was the principle that the limits of language are the limits of our world and *vice versa*. This principle obviously has some bearing on one central tenet of theism, namely the doctrine that God is transcendent. It raises the question: if, by definition, God lies beyond the limits of the world – and that, presumably, is what it means to call him 'transcendent' – can we speak meaningfully about him at all?

I think that we must first distinguish between some different senses in which God has been believed to be transcendent, i.e. more, or other, than the world.[28] According to one such sense, he is transcendent in that he is not a part of the spatio-temporal world. The latter is his creation and he is active within it, but he must not be identified with it or any part of it. According to another sense, God is transcendent in that his activities and qualities surpass those of other beings whom we observe or may imagine. He is infinitely creative, infinitely wise, infinitely loving, etc. According to a third sense, God is transcendent in that he is inconceivable. He is what we cannot (logically) think or say. He is what is self-contradictory or logically impossible.

There are, no doubt, other senses in which theists have affirmed God to be transcendent, but these three will suffice to indicate two main aspects of the problem of divine transcendence. One is: does it make sense to speak of God as transcendent in the first or second of our senses? The difficulty here is how we are to conceive of a divine agent who has no physical body. The other aspect of the problem is: does it make sense to speak of God as transcendent in the third of our three senses? Here what we need to understand is how the concept of transcendence is limited by that of logical possibility. I will deal with these two aspects of the problem in reverse order.

In a contribution to a philosophical conference, held a few years ago in New York, Paul Tillich contended that God is transcendent in the sense that the symbol 'God' is '. . . a representation of that which is unconditionally beyond the conceptual sphere.' He went on to explain that 'the word "God" produces a contradiction in the consciousness, it involves something figurative that is present in the consciousness and something not figurative that we really have in mind and that is represented by this idea'. He adds that 'the word "God" has the peculiarity of transcending its own conceptual content – upon this depends the numinous character that the word has ...'[29]. Tillich was not here saying that a mystic, for instance, might know God by acquaintance, but be unable to describe him. That is perfectly conceivable. But Tillich is saying, in effect, that we can know what we do not know. And that, surely, is nonsense. How is it logically possible for a word to transcend its own conceptual content? How is it logically possible to conceive of that which lies unconditionally beyond the conceptual sphere? Tillich recognized that this would constitute 'a contradiction in the consciousness', but he evidently thought that it nevertheless makes sense to say that we can have such an idea.

The reason which he would, presumably, have given for saying that we can, is : because God is God. That is to say, because God is, in some way, above or beyond logic; and so self-contradictory assertions may be significantly made of him. This is not so. To deny that it is so is not to say that God is, in any way, limited. It is simply to point out that assertions such as 'God both is and is not X' or 'God can make an X which both is and is not Y' do not assert anything. To assert anything necessarily is to differentiate what is the case from what is not. The trouble with self-contradictory assertions is that they are logically compatible with anything at all being the case, and so fail to meet this necessary condition of significant assertion.

Consider the following perfectly valid piece of reasoning :

> P and not P
> If P, then P or R
> But not P (From initial assertion)
> Therefore R.

The initial assertion is a contradiction. R, the conclusion, may be any statement at all, and yet the deduction be valid. Now consider the following:

> I know God whom I do not know
> If I know God, then either I know God or you are a poached egg
> But I do not know God (From initial assertion)
> Therefore you are a poached egg.

In this case, as in the foregoing, the conclusion, absurd though it is, follows validly from the initial assertion. The point to notice is that *any* other statement whatever which we choose to write instead of 'You are a poached egg' would also follow validly, even though the initial assertion is about God.

It is quite clear that the answer to the question: does it make sense to speak of God as transcendent in the sense of self-contradictory? is that it does not. If this be so, there are only two courses open to the rational theist. He may hold that theism without a self-contradictory God would not be genuine theism, and, in that case, he must abandon theism as an absurdity. Alternatively, if he holds that all which is vital to theism in the concept of divine transcendence can be stated without self-contradiction, then he need only keep clear of those dubious friends of theism who insist upon making self-contradictory statements about God.

I think a concept of God, which is compatible with all that is essential in theistic belief and which retains what Tillich called 'the numinous character' of the word, can be worked out, if God is taken to be transcendent simply in the sense that he is very mighty, very merciful and very mysterious. These latter are all perfectly intelligible expressions. It makes quite good sense to say that what God is, or does, amounts to more than we observe, or imagine, or can explain. The beliefs which are held concerning God, and the attitudes which are deemed appropriate towards him – at any rate if we are thinking of theism as it is represented by the Bible – have found an adequate grounding in such a concept of God as I have just proposed. I see no reason whatever for the view that, in order to be the God of theism, God must be such that self-contradictory assertions can be made about him.

The other aspect of the problem of divine transcendence which we noted above – namely : does it make sense to speak of God as transcendent in the senses of being part of the physcal world or being surpassingly loving, etc.? – is not so easy to dismiss. The difficulty, as we noted, lies in conceiving of God as an agent who has no spatio-temporal body.[30]

To see part of the difficulty here, we may take the restatement of 'God is loving', which Cox proposed in the article mentioned above. It ran: 'some experiences called "meeting God" will probably be experiences of meeting a person who loves you'. Three words here are puzzling : 'meeting', 'person', 'loves'. They are puzzling in the following way. We know well enough what would be meant if someone talked of *meeting* Bill Smith. One element in such a meeting, whatever else it involved, would be physical – they would sense Bill's body in some way – see or touch him, hear his voice on the phone, feel him pulling on the end of a rope, or whatever. Would it not be odd if anyone said that he had met Bill Smith in the total absence of this 'sensing the body' element?

Again, we know well enough what it means to say that Bill Smith is a *person*. Each person is, no doubt, more than his physical body, but his body is essential to his being a person, as we normally understand this latter word. Would it not be odd to say, 'I met an interesting person today. Bill Smith. He had no body !' Are ghosts, shades, poltergeists persons ? Surely not ! Yet they do have 'bodies' of a sort. What it would be like for anyone to be a person and have no body at all is quite inconceivable.

Yet again, we know what it would mean to say that Bill Smith *loves* Mary Smith. It would mean somewhat different things, according to whether she was his mother, his wife, or his popsy ; but in each case there would be spatio-temporal events, involving Bill Smith's body, which formed part of what 'loves' meant. What sense could it make to say that Bill Smith loves Mary Smith, whom he has never seen, heard, spoken or written to, touched, or had any physical contact with? Is it not impossible to conceive of what such 'loving' could be?

The point, then, is that Bill Smith's physical body would be an essential element in what anyone meant who spoke of Bill Smith as a person you can meet who loves you. Cox spoke of God as a person we meet who loves us. If he was referring – as he plainly was – to the God of theism, who is transcendent in the sense that he has no spatio-temporal body, then what I called the ' "sensing the body" element' cannot be part of what Cox meant by 'meet', 'person', or 'loves', when he applied these words to God. What, then, can he be taken to have meant by these words?

We cannot dispose of the difficulty simply by claiming that God is a different sort of being from Bill Smith. He may well be. But the point at issue is the intelligibility of the statements which we wish to make about God. If we want to use words such as 'meeting', 'person' or 'loves' with reference to God, then what we say only makes sense if we can attach clear meanings to these words. Could you form any clear conception of what it would mean to say that you had met a person who loves you, where *ex hypothesi* the being to whom you were referring had no physical body? Think of anything which you could conceive of, as meant by these words, and do you not find that the presence, and usually the movement, of the referent's physical body is presupposed?

The traditional way out of the difficulty is, of course, to say that such words as 'loves' are used analogically, or symbolically, of God. But I find it hard to make much sense of a great deal that theologians have written about analogy and symbol. They recognize that the meaning of such a word as 'loves' is clear enough, when man is the subject of the verb. They see – as they must – that there is a logical gap between what it means in such case and what it means when God is the subject of the verb. They realize that this gap in meaning must, in some way, be bridged if, in their talk of God, they are not to fall into meaninglessness by using language when an element, or elements, essential to its meaning is lacking. And it is at this point that they talk of analogy or symbol as constituting the necessary bridge. But, in the last analysis, what their talk of analogy or symbol always seems to amount to is no more than that they have bridged the gap in meaning by some flash of insight or intuition. What I find it hard to see is how 'bridging the gap by insight or intuition' amounts to anything more than simply 'jumping the gap'. When it comes to issues of meaning, you cannot just go around jumping gaps; if you are to get over them at all you must build logical bridges which make it perfectly clear that the sense in which you are using language is an intelligible one.

The question of the relationship between an agent and his body is notoriously difficult. On the one hand, as I have tried to show, it seems to make no sense to say that an agent *loves*, for example, where there is neither presence nor movement of the agent's physical body. Yet, on the other hand, as some contemporary philosophers[31] have clearly shown, the concept of agency cannot be reduced to that of bodily movement. There are important logical distinctions between the two.

To illustrate the sort of distinction which I have in mind here, let us suppose that a man, Smith, takes hold of Mrs. Jones' shopping basket. What is happening? An answer in terms of spatio-temporal events, causally connected, could be constructed, showing how the movements of Smith's body and those of Mrs. Jones' basket are related. But, however complete such an answer became, a question would not necessarily have been answered, namely : what was Smith doing ? For instance, he may have been stealing the basket or he may have been giving Mrs. Jones a helping hand, and, in either case, the description of what was happening in terms of bodily movement could be the same. What occurred, in terms of agency, could be different in the two cases, and yet what occurred in terms of the movements of the agent's body be the same. This shows clearly that the concept of agency cannot logically be reduced to that of bodily movement.

But let us suppose that Smith was, in fact, stealing the basket. He is caught, convicted and publicly disgraced. Subsequently he is found to be suffering from kleptomania. These circumstances – his capture, conviction, disgrace and affliction with kleptomania – are aspects of what may be called Smith's *situation*. He is logically distinct from his situation. We can ask him what he is going to do about his situation. Notice that this question can as meaningfully take the form, 'What are you going to do about your kleptomania?' as 'What are you going to do about the fact that you are in disgrace?'. Even though the kleptomania is, so to say, 'in' Smith's body or mind, whereas the disgrace is not, they are both aspects of his situation. There is, at this point, no sharp line to be drawn between Smith's body and the rest of his situation, such that the latter can be intelligibly regarded as logically distinct from Smith, as agent, but not the former. Smith, as agent, is systematically elusive to both. He is, therefore, as agent, not logically identifiable with his body.

What I venture to suggest is that such distinctions as I have drawn in the case of Smith may be applied to God as agent; and that they go some little way towards helping us with our problem of how God can intelligibly be said to be transcendent in the sense of having no spatio-temporal body.

Before trying to indicate just how I think they might help, there are two points which I readily concede. First, God cannot logically be a person, if he is transcendent in the sense of having no body, because persons do have bodies. Second, it may well be that acts of God cannot be said to have occurred, where nothing whatever, describable in terms of spatio-temporal events, causally connected, has occurred. I would simply add, on the first of these concessions, that it is surely not necessary for a theist, as such, to believe that God is a person, only that he is an agent; and, on the second, that I do not think any theist would wish to say that God had acted – in the spatio-temporal universe, that is – where nothing describable in terms of spatio-temporal events, causally connected, had occurred.

Very tentatively, I wish to hazard the following argument. I take it as granted that any agent is logically distinct from his situation in the way which I have illustrated; and that, where an agent, such as Smith, has a body, this may legitimately be thought of as part of his situation. I infer that the concept of an agent without a body is intelligible.

Against this inference, it could be pointed out that two things can be logically distinct, yet one be the necessary condition of the other. Smoke is logically distinct from fire, but there is no smoke without fire. So, it will be argued, we have not proved, simply by showing agency to be logically distinct from bodily movement, that agency can occur in the absence of bodily movement. But, in reply to this – to take the smoke and fire example – by saying that fire is a necessary condition of smoke, we should not mean that we could not conceive of smoke, without conceiving also of fire; we should simply mean that smoke, in our experience, is caused by fire, and possibly, also, that we could not imagine anything else which might cause it. But this is not to deny that there may be such a cause. Whether there is or not will be a matter for inquiry. We do not have to presuppose that there is no such cause in order to understand the concept of smoke. May we not then say similarly that, although, in our experience of human agents, agency does not occur without movement of the agent's body, and although we may be unable to imagine what it would be like to be an agent without a body, nevertheless, we do not have to presuppose bodily movement in order to conceive of agency?

If, as I have contended, an agent is systematically elusive to his body – in the sense that, whatever has been said in terms of bodily movement, it can always make sense to ask a question, which may be called one of agency, such as, 'What is the agent doing?' or 'What is he going to do about the fact that he is in this situation?' – does it not follow that agency is conceivable apart from bodily movement? If so, it is open to us to say that we can speak intelligibly of God as an agent without a body, even though we cannot imagine what it must be like to be God.

It is not, as I have conceded, open to us to say that God is a person because having a body is part of what it means to be a person. Nor is it open to us to say that God acts in the world when no spatio-temporal events occur. But as theists we need feel no compulsion to say such things.

I am not really satisfied with these arguments. At best, they seem to leave us with an ultimate dualism between what is happening in terms of agency and what is happening in terms of a series of spatio-temporal events, causally connected. Agency and this series are related only in the sense that they occur concurrently and the question as to why this should be so remains a great mystery. All I would venture to say is that, if this is an unsatisfactory position, it is so with regard to Smith as well as to God. The mere fact that Smith has a body, whilst God has not, does not solve the problem, so far as Smith is concerned, because Smith's body is part of his situation. In both cases – God and Smith – the logical gap between agent and situation remains. It is, however, something to have shown – if one has succeeded in doing so – that there is no particular problem concerning God at this point. The relation between God's agency and what goes on in the world is not unintelligible– as against the relation between Smith's agency and what goes on in the world which is intelligible – simply because God is transcendent is the sense of having no body. If there are difficulties in the way of making the relation between agency and what goes on in the world intelligible, they apply just as much to Smith's agency as to God's.

6

Later Thought

"Critique of the *Tractatus*"

IN the *Tractatus*, Wittgenstein had tried to show that 'a proposition has one and only one complete analysis' (3.25). In *Philosophical Investigations*, he subjected this 'picture theory' to damning criticism. We will note one or two of the defects which he found in it.

(i) To say that a word has no meaning when nothing corresponds to it is to confuse the meaning of a name with the bearer of the name. 'When Mr. N. N. dies, one says that the bearer of the names dies, not that the meaning dies. And, it would be nonsensical to say that, for if the name ceased to have meaning, it would make no sense to say "Mr. N. N. is dead".'(40)[32]

(ii) It makes no sense to speak of an *absolute* one-one correspondence between the simples of language and those of reality, as the picture theory required, because it makes no sense to speak of breaking reality down *absolutely* into its simples. For instance, you could conceivably break down the visual image of a tree into all the different colours of which it is composed; or, alternatively, into all the tiny straight lines of which its outline is composed. Now, which are its simple constituent parts – the colours or the lines? Multi-colouredness is one kind of complexity; being made up of tiny straight lines is another. 'We use the word "composite" (and therefore the word "simple") in an enormous number of different and differently related ways'. (47). Questions which suppose *absolute* complexity and simplicity, quite apart from context, are unanswerable.

(iii) Wittgenstein pointed out that the meaning of a proposition does not necessarily become clearer when it is analysed into more elementary propositions. If someone said, not 'The broom is in the corner' but 'The broomstick is in the corner and the brush is in the corner and the broomstick is fixed in the brush' his hearers would not understand him better; they would wonder why he was talking in such an odd, roundabout way (60).

(iv) The picture theory had assumed that a proposition is meaningless, if it does not have an absolutely determinate sense. But, said Wittgenstein, 'If I tell someone "Stand roughly here" – may not this explanation work perfectly – And cannot every other one fail too?' (88). 'Roughly' constitutes a refusal to say exactly to what place the speaker is referring, yet we can understand what he means. Other explanations could 'fail' in the sense that, however precisely you told someone where to stand he could always ask you to be more exact.

(v) Wittgenstein had said in the *Tractatus* that we correlate the propositional sign with that which it signifies by intending it to have that reference: by 'thinking the sense of the proposition' (3.11). Meaning is given to the proposition by a mental act distinct from uttering the sign. So far as meaning is concerned, therefore, the sign is arbitrary. But now Wittgenstein said: 'Make the following experiment: *say* "It's cold here" and *mean* "It's warm here". Can you do it?' (510). No. But though it would certainly not make sense to say that one had done it simply by thinking or intending 'warm' as one said 'cold', we could reply to Wittgenstein that it would make quite good sense to say that one had invented a game or code in which 'It's cold here' meant what is normally meant by 'It's warm here'. And on that point we can pass to the positive things which Wittgenstein had to say about meaning in the *Investigations*.

Language-Games

The view of meaning which Wittgenstein expounds in the *Investigations* may be roughly expressed as that the meaning of a word or sentence is the use to which it is normally put. In order to know the meaning we must ask, not : what does this picture ?, but : what job does this do ? Wittgenstein imagines a situation in which the bare essentials of language are realized. 'A is building with building stones : there are blocks, pillars, slabs and beams. B has to pass the stones, and that in the order in which A needs them. For this purpose they use a language consisting of the words "block", "pillar", "slab", "beam". A calls them out ; – B brings the stone which he has learnt to bring at such-and-such a call. Conceive this as a complete primitive language.' (2) Now, the illuminating question is : what will B need to understand in order to understand what A *means* when, for example, the latter says 'Slab'?

He will need to know three things, at least. (i) What naming is. 'Slab' names a type of object. B must have learned to ask, 'What is that called ?' and to interpret the word 'slab' as an answer to this question. (27). (ii) B must know what it is which 'slab' names. A may ostensively define the word for him by pointing to a slab ; but notice that, if the slab to which A pointed were, say, rectangular or white, B might think that 'slab' was the name for rectangular or white objects and when A uttered this word, pass him, say, a rectangular piece of wood or a white tile. The ostensive definition can always be variously interpreted, said Wittgenstein, and B has to learn the correct interpretation (28). (iii) B must know what to *do*, when A says , 'Slab'. He must *see the point* of A's utterance. A is not simply saying 'Slab' in order to name an object, but to get one passed, and B does not understand him unless he has learned that this is what A means.

The important consideration, in all three cases, is that B needs what Wittgenstein calls 'training'. That is, partly training in the uses to which words are put in such linguistic activities as questioning, naming, commanding, etc.; and partly training in activities with which words are, to use Wittgenstein's word, interwoven, such as obeying a command. In other words, learning a language is learning to play what Wittgenstein called a 'language-game'. He defined a language-game as a 'whole, consisting of language and the actions into which it is woven' (7).

Words are like pieces in chess and 'the meaning of a piece is its role in the game' (563). This conception of language-games is said to have come suddenly to Wittgenstein as he watched a football match and realized that what the players were doing with the ball is what we do with words. We pass words to and fro in certain 'wholes', or activities, each of which has its own 'rules' and its own 'point', just as chess or football has. You need some training in order to understand the rules and the point of what is going on in the one case as in the other. And, in each case, there is a difference also between, so to say, players and spectators. For instance, the moralist, who uses words like 'right' and 'ought', in a first-order way, to chide or exhort, is a 'player'; the moral philosopher, who engages in the second-order activity of trying to understand what the rules and the point of moral discourse are, is a 'spectator' in this language-game. But the philosopher can only understand morality by watching what the moralist does with words, just as the spectator can only understand soccer by watching what players do with the ball ('watching' here including reading or hearing about it).

Wittgenstein believed that he had been wrong when he wrote the *Tractatus* because he had tried to impose on language preconceived ideas of what its meaning must be. Now he saw that what one ought to do is to 'look' at the actual uses to which words are put and learn from these (340). The first thing one learns, when one does so, is the enormous variety of such uses. Wittgenstein wrote: 'But how many kinds of sentences are there? Say assertion, question and command? – There are *countless* kinds: countless different kinds of use of what we call "symbols", "words", "sentences". And this multiplicity is not something fixed, given once for all, but new types of language, new language-games . . . come into existence and others become obsolete and get forgotten . . .' (23). And he proceeds to give a list of examples:

'Giving orders, and obeying them –
Describing the appearance of an object, or giving its
   measurements –
Constructing an object from a description (a drawing) –
Reporting an event –
Speculating about an event –
Forming and testing a hypothesis –
Presenting the results of an experiment in tables and
   diagrams –
Making up a story; and reading it –
Play-acting –
Singing catches –
Guessing riddles –
Making a joke; telling it –
Solving a problem in practical arithmetic –
Translating from one language into another –
Asking, thanking, cursing, greeting, praying.'

Two important points which he made about language-games
were: (i) ' . . . the term "language-*game*" is meant to bring into
prominence the fact that the *speaking* of language is part of an
activity, or of a form of life' (23); (ii) ' . . . what we do in our
language-game always rests on a tacit presupposition' (p.179).
We must try to see what he meant by 'form of life' and 'tacit
presupposition'.

To illustrate 'form of life', Pitcher quotes Wittgenstein's
curious remark: 'If a lion could talk, we could not understand
him' (p. 223) and then comments: ' . . . suppose a lion says
"It is now three o'clock" but without looking at a clock or his
wristwatch – and we may imagine that it would be merely a
stroke of luck if he should say this when it actually *is* three
o'clock. Or suppose he says "Goodness, it is three o'clock; I
must hurry to make that appointment", but that he continues to
lie there, yawning, making no effort to move, as lions are wont
to do. In these circumstances – assuming that the lion's general
behaviour is in every respect exactly like that of an ordinary lion,

save for his amazing ability to utter English sentences – we could not say that he has *asserted* or *stated* that it is three o'clock, even though he has uttered suitable words. We could not tell what, if anything he has asserted, for the modes of behaviour into which his use of words is woven are too radically different from our own. We would not understand him, since he does not share the relevant forms of life with us.'[33] It is, of course, true that, in children's stories, there are animals which talk; but the whole point is that a Tiger Tim or a Yogi Bear behaves, not as tigers or bears do, but as human beings do.

To see what is meant by the 'tacit presupposition' of a language-game, consider the way in which we talk about physical objects, such as the moon. We speak of the latter as a continuous existent, e.g. we say 'The moon wasn't full last night. It will be in a week's time'. Yet our experience of it is discontinuous. But, in the language-game of natural science or common sense, it is 'tacitly presupposed' that statements concerning our discontinuous experience (the evidence of our senses) constitute valid grounds for statements concerning continuous existents (such as this physical object, the moon). If anyone questioned the validity of this move, we could not give him good scientific reasons for making it. We could only point out that science and common sense presuppose it and if he is not prepared to make it he will have to give up these language-games or forms of life.[34]

In the light of Wittgenstein's later thought, many contemporary philosophers conceive their first, if not exclusive, task, as philosophers, to be that of making clear the jobs which words do in different language-games : how these are related to, or distinct from, one another, on what presuppositions they are based, etc. They are concerned to analyse language and would claim that, in so doing, they can shed light on the main problems with which philosophy has always been concerned. There seem to be those – perhaps particularly amongst theologians – who consider that linguistic analysts have brought philosophy down in the world. From being sages or seers, who instructed men in the nature of ultimate reality, philosophers have become mere grammarians, splitting verbal hairs. This view is ridiculous. Ever since Socrates, it has been the role of the philosopher to help men clear their heads. What Wittgenstein showed was the fact, which once shown is obvious enough, that this is largely, if not entirely, a matter of getting language right. To be clear is to use words correctly, to be confused is to misuse them. What else could understanding conceivably be concerned with, if not words ? And understanding is the goal of philosophy.

Religious Belief

In Wittgenstein's published writings, there is not much to show how he applied his later philosophy to religious belief, though, if it exists, more from him on this subject may eventually be forthcoming from his literary executors. At present, pupils' notes of some lectures on the subject are available in *Lectures and Conversations* (ed. C. Barrett, Oxford, 1966) and these are the source of the quotations in this sub-section.

In these lectures, as one would expect, Wittgenstein emphasized the importance of training. The training needed to be in what he called the 'techniques' of religious belief. One example, which he discusses at some length, is belief in a Last Judgment. If a theist says, 'I believe in a Last Judgment' and an atheist says 'I do not', what is the nature of the disagreement between them ? Wittgenstein is surely correct in thinking that it is not simply a case of one predicting an empirically observable event and the other denying it.

Weight of empirical evidence for a prediction does not appear to be either a sufficient or a necessary condition of religious belief. A man may think the empirical grounds for predicting this event, the Last Judgment, overwhelming without being a religious believer. 'Suppose, for instance,' said Wittgenstein, 'we knew people who foresaw the future; made forecasts for years and years ahead ; and they described some sort of Judgment

Day. Queerly enough, even if there were such a thing, and even if it were more convincing than I have described . . . belief in this happening wouldn't be at all a religious belief' (p. 56). Again, a man may hold religious beliefs, whilst recognizing that the empirical evidence for them is comparatively small. 'This (*sc.* his religious belief) in one sense, must be called the firmest of all beliefs, because the man risks things on account of it which he would not do on things which are by far better established for him.' (p. 54).

If Wittgenstein is correct here, does it simply mean that people are not reasonable where religious belief is concerned? His answer is that, in one sense of the word, they are unreasonable, but not in another.

'I would say, they are certainly not reasonable, that's obvious.

' "Unreasonable" implies, with everyone, rebuke.

'I want to say: they don't treat this as a matter of reasonability.

'Anyone who reads the Epistles will find it said: not only that it is not reasonable, but that it is folly.

'Not only is it not reasonable, but it doesn't pretend to be.' (pp. 57-8).

In what sense is religious belief unreasonable and, in what sense, not?

It is unreasonable in the sense that religious believers, as such, do not – or, at least, do not always – reason about their beliefs in the same way as scientists or historians do about their theories. It is true, of course, that religious people frequently invoke their own, or others', experiences, or point to some putatively historical event, in support of their convictions; but what they sometimes take to be good evidence here would not be so regarded in science or history. Wittgenstein instanced a man who said that he *knew* the Last Judgment would occur, and what it would be like, because he had seen it all in a dream. If this kind of thing is allowed to count as evidence that he knew, then knowledge must mean something very different in religion from what it means in science or history.

But it does not follow from this that religious belief is unreasonable in a pejorative sense. 'Why shouldn't one form of life culminate in an utterance of belief in a Last Judgment?', asked Wittgenstein rhetorically (p. 58). Those whom he did consider unreasonable, in a sense implying rebuke, were apologists for, or against, religion who made the 'ludicrous' assumption that religious beliefs can be corroborated, or refuted, by treating them as though they were scientific hypotheses. Referring to an attempt by one, Father O'Hara, (in a symposium *Science and Religion*, London, 1931) to show that religious beliefs can be scientifically proved, he said: 'I would definitely call O'Hara unreasonable. I would say, if this is religious belief, then it's all superstition.' (p. 59). On the other hand he contended that those who dismiss religious belief because it cannot be scientifically proved are absurdly supposing that religious believers are simply making 'blunders' in a kind of thinking which is essentially the same as that of scientists or historians. Sometimes, it is true, this is what they may be doing. If the traditional argument from design for instance, is taken as religious thinking, then here we have an appeal to empirical evidence (the order in the universe) in support of a hypothesis (that the universe was created by an intelligent being) which looks very similar to the way in which a scientist would appeal to empirical evidence in support of, say, the theory of gravitation. And it can, no doubt, be shown that the argument from design, if this is what it amounts to, is a blunder, or series of blunders. But much religious thinking is not of this kind and does not pretend to be. In that case, whatever objections you bring against it, it is not enough simply to say that the believer is making what, in science, would be blunders. Referring to the man who believed in a Last Judgment because he had dreamt about it, Wittgenstein said: 'If you compare it with anything in Science which we call evidence, you can't credit that anyone could soberly argue, "Well, I had this dream ... therefore ... Last Judgment".

You might say : *"For a blunder, that's too big"*. If you suddenly
wrote numbers down on the black-board, and then said : "Now
I'm going to add" and then said : "2 and 21 is 13", etc., I'd say :
"This is no blunder". ' (pp. 61-2, italics mine). The point here is
that it is just as foolish to think that you can dispose of religion
simply by pointing out that it is bad science as it is to think that
you can prove it by claiming it to be good science.

According to Wittgenstein, what would count as indubitable
evidence in science or history is not enough in religion. Enough
for what ? The answer indicates his conception of the nature of
religious belief : ' . . . the indubitability wouldn't be enough to
make me change my whole life' (p. 57). In precisely what way
does religion change one's whole life ? He put it thus :

'Suppose somebody made this guidance for life : believing
in the Last Judgment. Whenever he does anything, this is
before his mind. In a way, how are we to know whether to
say he believes this will happen or not ?

'Asking him is not enough. He will probably say he has
proof. But he has what you might call an unshakeable belief.
It will show, not by reasoning or by appeal to ordinary
grounds for belief, but rather by regulating for in all his life.'
(pp. 53-54).

Believing in a Last Judgment does not mean – or not simply –
thinking it highly probable that a certain future event will occur.
'Here believing obviously plays much more this role : suppose we
said that a certain picture might play the role of constantly
admonishing me, or I always think of it. Here, an enormous
difference would be between those people for whom the picture
is constantly in the foreground, and others who just didn't use it
at all.' (p. 56). Religious belief, then, is *using a picture* – letting it
regulate your whole life, having it constantly in the foreground
of your thinking.

The kind of thing which Wittgenstein had in mind here could,
I think, be illustrated from the case of Carlyle. He put it on
record that, as he sat in Mrs. Austen's drawing-room with

Sidney Smith guffawing and other people prating, jargoning, 'to me through these thin cobwebs Death and Eternity sate glaring'. 'How will this look in the Universe and before the Creator of Man?' he asked himself. This picture of man as under judgment came through to him, not only in momentous events, but in trivial or commonplace situations no less. Asked in old age, 'Who will be judge?' he answered, 'Hell fire will be judge, God Almighty will be the judge now and always'.[35]

The technique of using the picture has to be acquired. Take Wittgenstein's example: 'God's eye sees everything'. To indicate what was meant by technique, he asked: ' . . . what conclusions are you going to draw? etc. Are eyebrows going to be talked of, in connection with the Eye of God?' (p. 71). God with an eye – that is the picture. But the question, 'Does God have bushy eyebrows?' will strike a religious man as ridiculous. That is not how he uses the picture. On the other hand, the question, 'Is God's eye sharp enough to count the hairs on every man's head?' will not seem silly to him. He will say that the answer is 'Yes'. That is how he does use the picture.

What emerges concerning the nature of the disagreement between religious believers and unbelievers? Wittgenstein said:

'If you ask me whether or not I believe in a Judgment Day, in the sense in which religious people have belief in it, I wouldn't say: "No. I don't believe there will be such a thing." It would seem to me utterly crazy to say this.
'And then I give an explanation: "I don't believe in . . ."
but then the religious person never believes what I describe.
'I can't say. I can't contradict that person.' (p. 55)

The point here, so far as one can see, is this. If an unbeliever is asked what he *means* by 'I don't believe in a Last Judgment' his answer will be that, on the available empirical evidence he does not think it probable that some predicted event – say, the return of Christ in two thousand years to judge the quick and the dead – will in fact occur. That is to say, he does not believe in it in the same way as he may not, for instance, believe in the destruction of civilization by atomic war before the end of the century. But, when the religious person says 'I believe in a Last Judgment', by 'I believe' he does *not* necessarily mean 'I think that there is what would be considered in science or affairs good empirical grounds for saying that something will happen'; he may, as we noted, say that he believes in it because he has dreamt about it. And by 'a Last Judgment' he does *not* mean – or not simply – some future event of the same kind as the destruction of civilization, because, as was said above, he could believe in the probability of the Last Judgment, as an event of that kind, without being a religious believer. This, then, is the sense in which believer and unbeliever cannot contradict one another. If A says 'I believe X' and B says 'I do not believe X', they can only be contradicting one another, if they mean the same by 'believe' and 'X'. Religious believers and unbelievers do not.

The disagreement between them is more fundamental. What it comes to is that they use different pictures – or that the believer uses a picture and the unbeliever does not. This is how Wittgenstein put it:

'Suppose someone is ill and he says: "This is a punishment." and I say: "If I'm ill, I don't think of punishment at all". If you say: "Do you believe the opposite?" – you can call it believing the opposite, but it is entirely different from what we would normally call believing the opposite.

'I think differently, in a different way. I have different pictures' (p. 55).

This can perhaps be illustrated by recalling Professor R. M. Hare's reply to Flew on 'Theology and Falsification'.[36] Hare contended that religious belief is having a *blik*. He illustrated what he meant by *blik* from the case of a lunatic who thinks all dons wish to murder him. The lunatic will not accept any evidence as falsifying his belief about dons: if they are kind to him he interprets this as diabolical cunning intended to put him off-guard. Being unfalsifiable, his *blik* may be said – following

Flew (see above p. 29) – to assert nothing. But it nevertheless makes a world of difference between him and those who do not share it because it determines what, for him, is, and what is not, an explanation. 'Diabolical cunning' explains the good deeds of dons; 'goodwill' would not. Hare brings out the all-important point that sane men, besides lunatics, have *bliks*. Anybody who undertakes to explain anything must have one. He must, that is, have a way of looking at the world which will determine what, for him, is an explanation and what is not. Suppose for instance that his *blik* is the uniformity of nature – he sees the world as a system in which like causes always have like effects. Then he will not be satisfied with any explanation which supposes an event to have occurred without the effect, which it has always previously been observed to cause, following.

The religious believer, as such, has his picture – or pictures – his *blik*, his way of looking at the world. If he believes in a Last Judgment, for instance, his account of everything which men do will, in the last analysis, be in terms of reward or punishment, here or hereafter, at the hands of a righteous, Divine Judge. Nothing will count for him, *qua* believer in a Last Judgment, as an explanation of human actions which does not answer the question: 'How will this look in the Universe and before the Creator of man?'

It is important to notice that Wittgenstein seems to have been at some pains to make it clear, in his lectures, that he did not consider his account of religion to discredit it. With reference to the view that the believer uses a picture, he said: 'I don't want to belittle him', and again: 'I don't want to say anything he himself wouldn't say' (p. 79). He evidently thought that it did not follow from anything which he had said that religion is false, childish or absurd. And he apparently thought that a believer, who recognized himself to be using a picture, would find this perfectly compatible with everything which, *qua* believer, he already said or did. Is there good reason to agree with Wittgenstein on these two counts? Is it, for instance, enough to show that religious belief is using a picture; does not one have to go on and show that this picture corresponds to something in objective reality? To such questions we shall return in Section 7.

Philosophical Perplexity

In the *Investigations*, Wittgenstein defined philosophy as 'a battle against the bewitchment of our intelligence by means of language' (109). There are at least two ways in which the evil spell can be cast. (i) We may be 'held captive by a picture' – i.e. not simply a visual image, but a certain way of thinking about things. (ii) We may confuse what he called 'surface grammar' and 'depth grammar' – the former is the way a word is used in the construction of the sentence; the latter is, putting it roughly, the *point* of the language-game or form of life in which it plays a part (664: cf. what he says in the *Tractatus* about confusing the real and apparent logical form of a proposition (4.0031)).

Philosophical problems arise as a result of this bewitchment. Suppose, for instance, that, when we think of time we are held captive by the picture of it as a kind of thing – say, a stream – then we shall be puzzled about what sort of stream time is, about whether it had a beginning, etc. Or suppose, because 'This is right' (in a moral sense) is, on the surface, grammatically similar to 'This is red', we conclude that 'right', like 'red', is the name of some property which the subject of the sentence has – then we shall worry our heads with questions like: what sort of property is rightness?, how is it perceived?, etc. What is happening in such cases, Wittgenstein said, is that language has 'gone on holiday' or 'is idling' (38:132). To understand a word or sentence, you must see it at home, or at work – that is, playing its part in its appropriate language-game or form of life. Questions about time do not belong among those about streams; nor does talk about the morality of actions belong in discussions about the properties of things.

Though Wittgenstein did not use them, we may take the demand that theological propositions shall be empirically falsifiable and the contention that moral properties are intuited as typical illustrations of what he meant by philosophical perplexity arising from confusion.

I tried to show above that the former is, in effect, a demand that theological propositions shall conform to the rules, and fulfil the point, of scientific hypotheses. But 'How is this religious belief to be empirically falsified ?' is a pseudo-problem – like, 'How many runs did Bobby Charlton score in the World Cup ?'. And, unless you have decided in advance that cricket is the only game worth playing, the fact that this latter question is nonsensical does not imply that soccer is worthless. Nor does it follow that theological belief is meaningless or disreputable, if it is not scientific hypothesis. A pro- or anti- apologetic which supposes that it does, is simply wrong-headed.

So long as the meaning of all moral language is taken to be its referent, it does follow that such a word as (morally) 'right' must either be meaningless or refer to something. If it refers to something, we are landed with the philosophical problems of what this is and how we can know which actions have it and which do not. To the intuitionist solutions – that the property referred to is 'non-natural' and that we know it by a mysterious faculty of intuition – there are serious philosophical objections.[37] But the problems only arise because we have been held captive by a certain view of meaning, reinforced by the 'surface-grammatical' similarity between sentences (e.g. 'This apple is red', 'This act is right') in which moral and non-moral terms are used. Now let us ask what job moral language does, and the fog clears. In what typical circumstances do we use such language ? Not when we are describing states of affairs, or not that simply, but when we are commending or discommending states of affairs, exhorting to or dissuading from action, advising, persuading, grading, etc. Moral language is typically *evaluative* rather than merely descriptive ; and putting a price or value on something, or agreeing to it, is not the same sort of activity as identifying or describing a thing's properties. The philosophical questions to which theological or moral discourse gives rise are, of course, more complicated than this summary account may suggest, but enough has been said to illustrate what Wittgenstein meant by being trapped in, or bewitched by, a picture or a way of speaking.

It will be recalled that, in the *Tractatus*, he had said that 'philosophy aims at the logical clarification of thoughts' (4.112); and had spoken of the solution of some philosophical problems as consisting in the vanishing of the problem (6.521). There, by clarification, he meant analysis into simples; and by vanishing, vanishing into meaninglessness. In the *Investigations*, he said: ' . . . and the clarity we are aiming at is indeed *complete* clarity. But this simply means that the philosophical problem should *completely* disappear' (133.). The similarity with the *Tractatus* is real enough and here we have a thread which holds together, in some sense, Wittgenstein's earlier and later thought. But it should now be clear that, in this last quotation, he meant by 'clarity' putting language in its appropriate context and, by the disappearing of philosophical problems, he meant the disappearance of muddles about the job which the language in question typically does.

7

'Theology as Grammar'

THIS heading occurs only in a parenthesis in the *Investigations* : 'Grammar tells us what kind of object anything is. (Theology as grammar)' (373). To be a religious believer, whatever else it may mean, is to participate in a language-game or universe of discourse. If the belief in question is theistic, this will involve talking about, or to, God and sharing in the experiences and activities connected with such discourse, which characterize the theistic form of life. Theology stands to religious belief, so understood, as its grammar does to a language. The grammar of any language reveals its logical structure. A language and its grammar could not exist independently of one another but working out, or learning, the grammar is distinct from using the language – for instance, knowing which mood the sentence 'A book is a good present' is in, or what is its subject and what its object, etc., is not the same thing as knowing that a book is a good present. Somewhat similarly, if religious belief did not exist, there would be no point in theology, but the two are not identical. Grammar has to show what it would, or would not, make sense to say in a language ; theology – and I include the most naive as well as the most sophisticated attempts to answer the whys and wherefors of those who reflect on religious belief – has to show what it does, or does not, make sense to say in a religion.

Following Wittgenstein, we spoke above of religious belief as using a picture. Theology has to do with what was called the 'technique' of using the picture. Just as a child learns to speak his native language before he is given lessons in its grammar, so, in religion, most people learn to use the picture before they concern themselves with questions which call for that clearer definition of technique which it is the theologian's job to provide. We will confine our discussion to theism, since that is a familiar form of religious belief. Suppose, for instance, that we have grown up using the picture of God as, without qualification, a good and powerful creator. We have been told stories which so describe him; and we have said prayers which assume that this is what he is. But now we begin to ask questions. For instance: then why are half the people in God's world hungry? Or, at a more sophisticated level: then why did there have to be an Atonement – if God is good why did he insist on a penalty being paid for sin, and if he is powerful, why did he not make men incapable of sin so that there would have been no occasion for a penalty? The theologian's task is to find answers to such questions. As we noted above, any man's *blik*, 'picture', or way of looking at the world, determines what, for him, does, and what does not, constitute an explanation. The Christian theologian has to work out explanations of world hunger, the Atonement, or whatever is in question, which are consistent with the Christian picture of God. In so doing, he has to take the picture as he finds it used by believers; but, at the same time, he has to define it, or the technique of using it, more clearly. If, for instance, he were to say that world hunger occurs because God does not care whether his creatures starve or not, this would be so inconsistent with the picture of God, which Christians use, that it would be quite unacceptable as an explanation. However, suppose our theologian were to say that world hunger is due to human selfishness; and go on to argue that God evinces his goodness in giving men freewill, but in so doing necessarily limits his power over them to that of persuasion. This explanation would define more precisely for some believers, what is meant by the goodness and power, attributed to God in the picture which they use.

Wittgenstein, I think, would have said that the philosopher of religion, like the theologian, is concerned with the technique of using the picture. The philosopher's task, however, is somewhat different from the theologian's. There are two aspects to it. (i) The philosopher must examine the guidance in using the picture, which the theologian gives, to see whether it is self-consistent or not. (ii) He must try to understand and reveal the 'depth grammar' of this technique.

The theologian's explanation of world hunger, suggested a moment ago, will serve to illustrate the first aspect of the philosopher's task. In saying that God evinces his goodness in giving men freewill, our theologian, presumably, purports to be taking 'goodness' and 'freewill' in their normal senses ; but is he, in fact, doing so, when he goes on to argue that this necessarily involves creating men who are capable of the selfishness which causes world hunger ?

At first blush, it seems that he is ; but closer scrutiny raises doubts. Take 'goodness'. There is, to say the least, something in the contention of those philosophers who point out that, if a man had to choose between producing a state of affairs, which would result in great suffering, and not producing anything at all, we should consider him good only if he chose the latter; and so, when our theologian claims that it is a mark of goodness in God to have created a world in which millions upon millions are starving, the word 'goodness' is being used in a very odd sense. Now take 'freewill'. Some philosophers recently have argued that it would not – as our theologian obviously supposes – be self-contradictory to say that God had given men freewill, in the normal sense of that word, and at the same time made them incapable of selfishness. 'Having freewill', as normally used, means : not being under certain kinds of compulsion, not doing what you do because, for instance, you are pushed, or intimidated, or ignorant of what you are doing, etc. In other words, 'freewill' means that the agent concerned does what *he* wills to do; he is *self-determined*. But there is nothing logically impossible in the idea of a man who is so made that, when he does what he wills to do, he always does what is unselfish. If God had made all men like that, they could (logically) have had freewill, in the sense of doing only what they willed to do, and at the same time been incapable of the selfishness which causes world hunger. Our theologian's assumption that this is self-contradictory is not in accordance with the normal sense of 'freewill', though that is the sense in which he purports to be using the term.

I am not saying that these arguments are conclusive against our theologian's explanation of evils like world hunger; and elsewhere I have tried to say why.[38] Here it is not necessary to take the discussion further. Enough has been said to show what was meant by describing the first aspect of the philosopher's task as that of examining for consistency the theologian's 'grammar', that is, his explication of the technique of religious belief.

The second aspect of the philosopher's task, we said, was to understand, and reveal, the 'depth grammar' of this technique. I think that Wittgenstein would have said that this involves two things at least: (i) discovering the tacit presuppositions of religious belief, and (ii) mapping its logical frontiers.

As for the former, depth grammar can show us 'what kind of object' God is. It will be remembered that Wittgenstein said this was its purpose: 'to show us what kind of object anything is'. The concept of God is constitutive of theistic belief and theology in the way that the concepts of number, obligation or a physical object are constitutive of arithmetic, morality and natural science respectively. As R. G. Collingwood insisted, everything that is said is said in answer to a question and every question is based on some presupposition(s).[39] Theism deals in questions and answers about God, and certain presuppositions about him are built into both the questions and the answers. When, for instance, Goethe asked, at the time of the Lisbon earthquake, 'Where is God and what is he doing?', he did not expect some such answer as 'Over there, standing next to the man in the red shirt, and wielding a shovel!' What he asked was to be shown some point in the earthquake which would make it consistent with the purpose of a God, whom both he and those who tried to answer him took to be good, but whom neither he nor they took to have a physical body. Presuppositions about the sense in which God can be conceived as an agent are built into the question and anything which would be intelligible as an answer to it. To reveal such presuppositions is to discover the internal logic of theism, or to 'show what kind of object' God is.

By mapping the logical frontiers of religious belief, I mean avoiding the confusions which arise from failure to mark off its questions and answers from those of other kinds. One such confusion is that of which apologists for or against religion are guilty when they take belief in God to be the same kind of logical thing as a scientific hypothesis. Another example is Professor P. van Buren's attempt in *The Secular Meaning of the Gospel* (London, 1963) to reduce theology (God raised Christ from the dead) to human psychology (The disciples experienced a new freedom). This is a paradigm case of the kind of logical frontier-violation which depth grammar must condemn. It is just muddle-headed to suppose that, when you say something about God what you 'really mean' is something about men. Of course, it does not necessarily follow that acts of God and human feelings cannot, in certain ways, be related; but for there to be a relation between them, they must (logically) be two things, not one.

A great many dilemmas, connected with religious belief, as I tried to show above in discussing theology and falsification and the problem of transcendence, can be resolved, when the character of religious discourse as *sui generis* is clearly recognized. A remark of Professor G. Ryle comes to mind : 'If the seeming feuds between science and theology . . . are to be dissolved at all, their dissolution can come not from making polite compromises but only from drawing uncompromising contrasts between their businesses.'[40] But, when we have discovered the tacit presuppositions and mapped the logical frontiers of religious belief, have we disposed of all the philosophical problems to which it gives rise?

The question raised above, at the end of our discussion of Wittgenstein's lectures on religious belief, has not been faced as yet. It is all very well to show, if one can, that theistic belief is a distinctive language-game, constituted by the concept of God. But does God really exist? It tells us much, maybe, to say that the religious believer uses a picture in accordance with a certain technique, but is this a picture of anything objectively real? The question seems to be not only legitimate but inescapable.

We must consider it now. Some modern philosophers, I think under the influence of the later Wittgenstein, would say that it rests on a misconception. Professor T. R. Miles in *Religion and the Scientific Outlook* (London, 1959) spoke of 'the absolute existence mistake'. He pointed out that we know well enough how to differentiate what exists from what does not, or what is real from what is unreal, in certain spheres. Take as examples the questions: 'Does the Loch Ness monster really exist?' 'Is six times thirty shillings really nine pounds?' 'Have children a real duty to support their parents in old age?', 'Is it really God's will that a penurious mother of six should not take "the pill"?'. There are techniques in natural science, arithmetic, ethics, and theology respectively for answering such questions. But how are we to deal with a question which concerns the reality or otherwise of the constitutive concept of a universe of discourse, e.g. 'Does the physical world really exist?' or 'Does God really exist?' Such questions – and any answers to them – presuppose that we can give an ontologically ultimate definition to 'really exists' and justify it, but can we? The matter is complex and I must content myself with making two points only here.

(i) 'Really exists' seems to be indefinable in somewhat the way that G. E. Moore said 'good' was.[41] Take *any* proposed definition of 'really exists', e.g. 'being part of the physical world'. If this definition is correct – i.e. if in normal use this is what 'really exists' means – notice what follows. The statement, 'What is part of the physical world really exists' must then appear to most people to be an insignificant tautology, equivalent to 'What is part of the physical world is part of the physical world'. And the question 'Does what is part of the physical world really exist' must appear self-answering, equivalent to 'Is what is part of the physical world part of the physical world?' However, is this how the statement and the question do appear? Would the reader say that 'What is part of the physical world really exists' seems to him a mere tautology, similar to 'Apples are apples'? Or would he say that the question, 'Does the physical world really exist?' can be answered simply by consulting an accurate dictionary, as the question, 'Is a bachelor an unmarried male?' can? I think not.

Materialists, most of all, have to agree with what I have just been saying. Their belief may be stated thus : if anything really exists, then it is part of the physical world. This belief is held in conscious opposition to various alternatives, e.g. that God, Platonic ideas, the Unconscious, or whatever, really exist. Materialists undoubtedly want the statement of their belief to be understood as ontologically significant and informative. But if 'really exists' meant 'being part of the physical world', the statement, 'If anything really exists, then it is part of the physical world' would be neither significant nor informative ontologically. All it would amount to is : if anything is part of the physical world, then it is part of the physical world. Materialists are misguided if they try to make their beliefs true by definition. Statements which are true by definition have to do only with the meanings of words. But materialists, as such, do not hold beliefs about the meanings of words, but about the nature of ultimate reality.

The point which I am making here does not, of course, apply only to materialistic definitions of 'really exists'. Suppose I believe that what really exists is God. Do I mean by this only what I would mean by 'God is God'? Surely not! And if some inquirer asked, 'But does God really exist?' should I reply 'My dear chap, you have only to look at your dictionary!'? *Whatever* X is taken to be, if 'X really exists' purports to be an ontologically significant and informative remark, then X cannot logically be the *definition* of 'really exists'. This is the sense in which I claim that 'really exists' is indefinable.

(ii) The second point which I want to make about 'really exists' arises from the fact that people sometimes talk as though it made sense to speak of getting outside all conceptual schemes whatsoever and discovering what really exists. But what would be involved in such an ontologically ultimate discovery and would it make sense to say that anyone had made it? Every conceptual scheme, I have claimed earlier, has its constitutive concept or concepts : science, that of a physical object; morality, that of obligation, etc. Suppose we say that it is not enough to know that these are the ultimate presuppositions of certain ways of thinking; we must find out which of them really exist and which do not. We might conceivably invent a conceptual scheme, distinct from science and morality, within which the questions, 'Do physical objects really exist?' and 'Does obligation really exist?', could both be asked and possibly answered. Let us call this metaphysical and metamoral scheme M. There will necessarily be some concept or concepts – perhaps one called the Absolute – which constitute, i.e. give its logical features to – M. But what if somebody wants to know whether the Absolute, in its turn, is not just the presupposition of a way of thinking, but really exists? We shall have to invent another scheme within which that question – together with those about physical objects and obligation – can intelligibly be asked and answered. But now : does the constitutive concept of this new scheme really exist? And so on. We are in an infinite regress.

To *know* anything we must be aware of it as something; and this is simply to say that we must think or speak of it in terms of some conceptual scheme – as a physical object, or a duty, or a mode of the Absolute, or whatever. This follows from the meaning of 'know'. We cannot therefore meaningfully say that we know anything outside any conceptual scheme whatsoever. Since it is nonsense to say that we have discovered something which we could not know, neither does it make sense to say that we had got outside all conceptual schemes and discovered what, in that sense, really exists.

I must emphasize that there are two things which *do not follow* from these two points which I have made about 'really exists'.

(i) Professor E. L. Mascall seems to think that, if we cannot do what I have said that we cannot – namely, define 'really exists' in an ontologically ultimate sense, or discover outside all conceptual schemes which of their constitutive concepts really exist and which do not – it must then be 'impossible to distinguish significantly between the existence or non-existence of anything : you can say significantly that the cat is on the mat, but you cannot say significantly whether it is a real or an imaginary cat to which you are referring'.[42] But of course you can! We know well enough what is normally meant by a real cat, as opposed to an imaginary one. Real cats meow, drink milk, squeal when trodden on, chase other cats on the tiles, etc. An imaginary cat is simply one which does not pass such tests. But if someone said that he knew a cat which was, in all these respects, just like a real cat, but was imaginary what should we make of that remark ? He would have, in effect, stepped outside the universe of discourse in which we normally differentiate real from imaginary cats. Within that universe his cat is a real one – it passes all the tests. What would he mean by calling it imaginary ? And how could he know that that was what it was ? If you say that he could not know, it does not follow for a moment, as Mascall evidently supposes, that the normal distinction between real and imaginary cats loses its significance.

(ii) Neither does it follow that, if we cannot know, apart from the presuppositions of the theistic conceptual scheme, that God really exists, the bottom is knocked out of theism. A thing which cannot be said is simply a thing which cannot be said. To say that the statement, 'I know outside any conceptual scheme that God really exists' would make no sense, is to say something about language but not necessarily about anything else. Compare that statement with this : God cannot do the logically impossible. People sometimes think that the latter denies the omnipotence of God, but it does nothing of the kind. It does not say anything about what God, in fact, can or cannot do. All it says is that, if anyone uttered the remark, 'God can do the logically impossible', he would be contradicting himself and so what he said would be meaningless. Similarly, if anyone said 'I have got outside all conceptual schemes whatsoever and away from their presuppositions, and discovered that what really exists is God', it would, in my opinion, be impossible to make any sense of what he said. But it does not follow from this that questions such as 'Is this really God's will?' or 'Does there exist in God an everlasting mercy?', and the answers which Christianity, for example, offers to them, do not make sense. These questions belong *within* the conceptual scheme of theism, and that is where answers to them will be found, if found at all. To say that they become insignificant, if a remark, which belongs outside that scheme altogether, is meaningless – namely, the one I quoted a moment ago about '. . . what really exists is God' – would be like saying that because God cannot do the logically impossible, he cannot do anything at all.

In the end, I think, we must say of religion in general, and theism in particular, what Wittgenstein said with wider reference. 'Our mistake is to look for an explanation where we ought to look at what happens as a "proto-phenomenon". That is, where we ought to have said: *this language-game is played*' (654). And again : 'What has to be accepted, the given, is – so one could say – *forms of life*' (p. 226). Like any other conceptual scheme, a religion is based logically upon presupposition, and is bounded logically by frontiers ; the former must be accepted, and the latter respected, if the game is to be played or the form of life taken up. In the case of theism, we must decide whether or not to deal in questions and answers which have to do with God. This decision is logically like deciding whether or not to do science, think morally, or take up some branch of mathematics. It is the decision to give, or not give, a certain frame to experience.

I think Wittgenstein would have agreed with this account of the matter, at any rate to some degree. He once said of his later philosophy : 'Its advantage is that if you believe, say, Spinoza or Kant, this interferes with what you believe in religion ; but if you believe me, nothing of the sort.' We have neither justified nor discredited theism in any ultimate sense. The difficulty is to conceive of what would be involved in doing so. There are, of course, all kinds of things to be said about theism: how it compares with other religions, what experiences are characteristic of it, what its theology of science, morality, history, is, etc. etc. But it would seem that it is an illusion to think that philosophy can do more than reveal its presupposition and draw its logical frontiers. That presupposition is God and those frontiers mark off talk about God from other kinds of talk.

It would, however, be dishonest to conceal the fact that, given this philosophical account of theism, there are still lingering philosophical questions which trouble one, as a theist. I can do little more than mention them here.

(i) How is talk about God to be differentiated logically from, say, talk about Santa Claus? Despite all that has been said above about 'really exists', this question persists. Surely God is believed by theists to be there – to be objective – in some sense in which Santa Claus is not! But in precisely what sense, and how does one show that he is, in a philosophically convincing way? Scientists test their theories by deducing from them empirically observable predictions. However conditioned their view of objective reality may be by the presuppositions of their science, they do commit their theories to 'what is there' and let them stand or fall by whether or not the predictions which they have deduced are fulfilled. When they are fulfilled, one can speak of the theory from which they have been deduced as 'knowledge', or as 'objectively true', in an intelligible sense. Objectivity here means being established in this way. But I have argued that religious beliefs are not to be treated as though they were scientific hypotheses. In what sense, then, do we speak of them as objectively grounded, i.e. as more than shared fantasies like that of Santa Claus? This seems to me to be the most urgent question confronting Christian philosophers today, but I must confess that I have not come upon any way of dealing with it which appears to me entirely satisfactory from a philosophical point of view.

(ii) How does one dispose of the contention that talk about God is unintelligible to modern man because it is obsolete?

Wittgenstein, it will be remembered, said that language-games may become 'obsolete and get forgotten'. Professor A. C. MacIntyre has recently argued that this is just what has happened to Christianity.[43] His point, if I rightly interpret it, is this. It will not do to say that understanding Christianity is simply a matter of accepting the presupposition(s) of a certain language-game or form of life and thinking or acting accordingly. One must consider what it involves for modern man to do so. When mediaeval man had to explain an occurrence or decide upon an action, the questions which he most naturally asked were, respectively, 'Why has God sent this upon us?' or 'What does God will us to do?' But these are not the questions which modern man naturally asks. He normally explains things, or decides upon action, in accordance with the presuppositions of natural science or utilitarian ethics. He can, of course, see that, *given* the presupposition of God, the above (mediaeval) questions make sense. But the point is that this is just a way of saying that he has to see how his normal criteria of intelligibility need to be changed in order to see how these questions make sense. To understand, for example, 'Why did God allow the Lisbon earthquake?', a modern man has to see how the answer to this differs from the way in which he normally explains earthquakes. So the normal way of explaining them in terms of natural cause and effect is still the determinative factor in understanding. For modern man, the criteria of intelligibility – even in the case of religious belief – are, in the last analysis, those of unbelief! In reply, two lines may be taken here. On the one hand, there is what might be called the 'fundamentalist' line : 'If modern man finds Christianity unintelligible, so much the worse for modern man!' On the other, the 'radical Christian' line : 'If the traditional presuppositions of Christianity are unintelligible to modern man, then we must replace them by those of natural science or utilitarian ethics and call these Christian!' But I find neither the move of the fundamentalist nor that of the radical Christian altogether satisfactory here.

(iii) The theistic language-game is played, but is it rational to take this game seriously? What constitutes rationality is, of course, a vexed question. But, to say the least, it is arguable that the rational man, as such, is the man who believes nothing unless he has good reasons for doing so, *and* who recognises that what appears to him a good reason today may, in the light of fuller knowledge, not do so tomorrow. In a word, he is a sceptic, though not an absolute one. He holds his beliefs, as it were, subject to modification. It is true enough, as preachers are fond of saying, that unbelievers must have faith of some kind just as much as believers: that, in order to think or act at all, they must presuppose the uniformity of nature, or the value of human happiness, or whatever. Nevertheless, the religious believer, as such, is committed to his presuppositions as the unbeliever is not, and as it is arguable that no rational man ought to be. Dr. W. W. Bartley has recently pointed out that the rationalist can remain a rationalist, whatever presupposition he finds himself compelled to abandon, but the Christian cannot remain a Christian and cease to believe that God has revealed himself in Jesus Christ.[44] There is, therefore, a limit to scepticism in the Christian position, which is not paralleled in that of the rational man, as such. Of course, one may simply reply to Bartley that, if that is how it is with Christianity, that is how it is; why should we be disturbed to find a Christian less sceptical than an unbeliever? But the worry is: does such a reply forfeit any claim to be taken seriously by the philosophically-minded unbeliever? Does it imply that Christianity is irrational?

These three questions take us, so to speak, to the front line of apologetics. Any adequate defence of Christian theism must take account of them. As I have indicated it is not easy to find convincing answers and work needs to be done by Christian thinkers on each of them.

They focus doubts about the view which has been put forward here that a body of religious belief, such as Christianity, must be regarded as a 'proto-phenomenon', that is, a form of life, or language-game, which neither requires nor admits of any justification beyond itself. But even if it should turn out that this view is the most that analytical philosophy can say about Christianity, I suggest that there is something important which might be added.

Some language-games, or forms of life, seem to be definitive of humanity in the sense that it is essential to our concept of man, as man, that he should engage in them. Morality would be a case in point. It is, I suppose, conceivable that men should cease to use moral language : that words such as 'right', 'good', 'ought', as they are now used in a moral sense, should drop out of our language. With them would go such activities as moral persuasion or argument ; and, no doubt, also such experiences as those which we call remorse or a sense of duty. I say that this is conceivable ; but when we imagine it, do we not have to add that, if it happened to *homo sapiens*, he would be deprived of something essential to what we have always meant by his humanity – in a real sense, he would cease to be man?

What I suggest, very tentatively, is that somewhat the same might be said of religious belief. It is true, of course that there are individuals who have no religious beliefs and, I am not for a moment disputing that many of them are admirable human beings. But could it be argued that there is a dimension, at once mysterious and magnificent, which religious language, and the kind of experience which goes with it, add to human life ; and that if this dimension were lost something essential to what we mean by calling our life 'human' would be lost also? Could it even be said that the unbeliever, who finds it necessary to argue about, or propagate, his unbelief, is witnessing to the impossibility of man, as man, ceasing to talk about God? 'This game is played'. But more : to play it is the nature of man.

Notes

1. *Philosophical Investigations*, 109.
2. 'Ludwig Wittgenstein', *Mind* 1951.
3. Biographical material from friends of Wittgenstein is to be found in : B. Russell, op. cit., G. Ryle, 'Ludwig Wittgenstein', *Analysis* 1951-52, G. E. M. Anscombe, 'What Wittgenstein Really Said', *The Tablet* 17.4.54, B. Russell, 'Philosophers and Idiots', *The Listener* 1955, K. Britton, 'Portrait of a Philosopher', ibid., N. Malcolm, *Ludwig Wittgenstein : A Memoir* (including a biographical sketch by G. H. von Wright) (London, 1958), E. Heller, M. O'C. Drury, N. Malcolm and R. Rhees, 'Ludwig Wittgenstein : A Symposium'. *The Listener* 1960.
4. *Mind* 1954, p. 78.
5. See note 3 above.
6. Cf. his *Lectures and Conversations* (edited by C. Barrett) (Oxford, 1966), p. 70.
7. See e.g. his *The World and God* (London, 1935), *God and Men* (London, 1948) etc.
8. *The Philosophy of Wittgenstein* (Englewood Cliffs, N. J., 1964).
9. The references in this section are to the Pears and McGuinness translation of the *Tractatus*. That work consists of seven main propositions, which Wittgenstein numbered 1 to 7. Explanatory comments are added upon each in accordance with a system of decimal numbering which Wittgenstein explained thus : 'The propositions *n*.1, *n*.2, *n*.3 are comments on proposition no. *n* ; the propositions *n.m*1, *n.m*2, etc. are comments on proposition no. *n.m* ; and so on.' (Op. cit., p. 7n.)
10. See Malcolm's *Ludwig Wittgenstein*, p. 78.
11. Cf. Pitcher, op. cit., p. 78.
12. For a discussion of this, see Pitcher, op. cit., pp. 83-86.
13. *Notebooks* 1914-16 (Oxford, 1961) 29.9.14 ; cf. *Tractatus* 4.031.
14. Cf. below p. 21.
15. Critical studies : G .E. M. Anscombe, *An Introduction to Wittgenstein's Tractatus* (second edition, London, 1963), M. Black, *A Companion to Wittgenstien's Tractatus* (Cambridge, 1964) E. Stenius, *Wittgenstein's Tractatus* (Oxford, 1964), J. Griffin, *Wittgenstein's Logical Atomism* (Oxford, 1964), J. Hartnack, *Wittgenstein and Modern Philosophy* (English translation, London, 1965), G. Pitcher, op. cit.
16. *Language, Truth and Logic* (second edition, London, 1946), p. 9.
17. This objection is noted by Ayer, op, cit. pp. 11-12.
18. Introduction to *Logical Positivism* (edited by Ayer) (Glencoe, Ill., 1959), p. 15.
19. E.g. Hartnack, op., cit. p. 41.
20. E.g. Anscombe, op. cit. p. 150.
21. Cf. Ayer, *Logical Positivism*, p. 16.
22. 5. 6. 15.
23. Introduction to the *Tractatus* (in Pears and McGuinness trans. p. xxi).
24. Black, op., cit. p. 386.

25. *New Essays in Philosophical Theology*, edited by A. Flew and A. MacIntyre (London, 1955) ; cf. J. Wisdom, 'Gods' in *Philosophy and Psycho-Analysis* (Oxford, 1957) (reprinted from *Proceedings of the Aristotelian Society*, 1944-45).

26. For a discussion, sympathetic to religion, of what is involved in other-than-logical truth-claims, see W. A. Christian, *Meaning and Truth in Religion* (Princeton, N. J., 1964).

27. 'The Significance of Christianity', *Mind*, 1950.

28. See my article on 'Transcendence' in *Theology* , March, 1966.

29. In *Religious Experience and Truth*, edited by S. Hook (New York, 1961), pp. 303, 315.

30. On this cf. P. Edwards, 'Some Notes on it. Anthropomorphic Theology' in Hook, op. cit.

31. E.g. see D. F. Pears (editor) *Freedom and the Will* (London, 1963).

32. The references in this section, unless otherwise stated, are to G. E. M. Anscombe's translation of Wittgenstein's *Philosophical Investigations* (Oxford, 1953). Those to Part I of that work are given by section ; those to Part II, by page.

33. Op. cit. p. 243.

34. Cf. P. F. Strawson on physical objects in his *Individuals* (London, 1959), p. 35.

35. I owe this reference to T. R. Glover's *The Jesus of History* (London, 1917), p. 148.

36. See Flew and MacIntyre, op. cit.

37. See my *Ethical Inutitionism* and G. J. Warnock's *Contemporary Moral Philosophy* (published by Macmillan).

38. 'An Attempt to Defend Theism', *Philosophy* 1964.

39. *Metaphysics* (Oxford, 1958).

40. *Dilemmas* (Cambridge, 1954), p. 81.

41. Cf. his *Principia Ethica* (Cambridge, 1903), chap. 1.

42. *The Secularization of Christianity* (London, 1965), p. 19n.

43. 'Is Understanding Religion Compatible with Believing?' in *Faith and the Philosophers*, edited by J. Hick (London, 1964).

44. *The Retreat to Commitment* (London, 1964).